THE INTERNET

SERIES IN UNDERSTANDING STATISTICS

S. NATASHA BERETVAS   Series Editor

SERIES IN UNDERSTANDING MEASUREMENT

S. NATASHA BERETVAS   Series Editor

SERIES IN UNDERSTANDING QUALITATIVE RESEARCH

PATRICIA LEAVY   Series Editor

Understanding Statistics

Exploratory Factor Analysis
Leandre R. Fabrigar and Duane
T. Wegener

Understanding Measurement

Item Response Theory
Christine DeMars

Reliability
Patrick Meyer

Understanding Qualitative Research

Oral History
Patricia Leavy

Fundamentals of Qualitative Research
Johnny Saldaña

The Internet
Christine Hine

CHRISTINE HINE

THE INTERNET

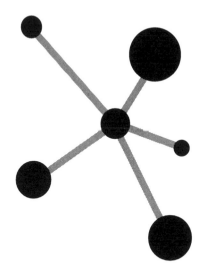

OXFORD
UNIVERSITY PRESS

OXFORD
UNIVERSITY PRESS

Oxford University Press is a department of the University of Oxford. It furthers
the University's objective of excellence in research, scholarship, and education by
publishing worldwide.

Oxford   New York
Auckland   Cape Town   Dar es Salaam   Hong Kong   Karachi
Kuala Lumpur   Madrid   Melbourne   Mexico City   Nairobi
New Delhi   Shanghai   Taipei   Toronto

With offices in
Argentina   Austria   Brazil Chile Czech Republic France Greece
Guatemala   Hungary   Italy   Japan   Poland   Portugal   Singapore
South Korea   Switzerland   Thailand   Turkey   Ukraine   Vietnam

Oxford is a registered trademark of Oxford University Press in the UK and certain other
countries.

© Oxford University Press 2013

Published in the United States of America by
Oxford University Press
198 Madison Avenue, New York, NY 10016

Library of Congress Cataloging-in-Publication Data
Hine, Christine.
    The Internet/Christine Hine.
       p. cm.—(Understanding qualitative research)
    Includes bibliographical references and index.
    ISBN 978-0-19-979389-1 (pbk.)
    1. Sociology—Research—Computer network resources.   2. Social sciences—
    Research—Computer network resources.   3. Qualitative research—Computer
    network resources.   4. Internet.   5. Report writing.   I. Title.
    HM571.H56 2012
    001.4'202854678—dc23   2012004643

9 8 7 6 5 4 3 2 1
Printed in the United States of America on acid-free paper

CONTENTS

THE INTERNET

1

INTRODUCTION

The Internet is the fabric of our lives.

—Castells 2002, p. 1

The Internet creates a crisis of boundaries between the real and the virtual, between time zones and between spaces, near and distant. Above all, boundaries between bodies and technologies, between our sense of self and our sense of our changing roles: the personae we may play or the "hats we wear" in different situations are altered.

—Shields 1996, p. 7

As qualitative researchers, we want to understand how people live their lives and make sense of what goes on around them. Very rapidly, the Internet has become a significant component of those lives; indeed, it often forms an unremarked part of the fabric of our everyday experience, as Castells (2002) describes. Checking a social networking site such as Facebook has become a routine activity that we may not think of in terms of "going on the Internet," but instead simply see as a way of keeping up with friends. Even as the Internet becomes so commonplace, however, commentators have expressed an enduring suspicion that maybe the Internet changes things, maybe it causes us to live our lives differently, or to be different people. For qualitative researchers wanting to understand the everyday, the Internet has therefore become almost unavoidable, but is also often troubling in the extent to which it seems to challenge our starting premises about who we study, where they are, and what they do there, as Shields (1996) describes. Although the Internet feels like familiar territory for many of the people we study, still it can seem quite strange and dangerous territory for a qualitative researcher.

This book focuses on the process of writing up qualitative Internet research. By choosing this particular focus, I intend to bridge the gulf between generic advice on academic writing and the specific challenges raised when writing about fieldwork on the Internet for an academic audience. Even though the Internet continues to embed itself ever more deeply into our everyday (and academic) lives, it is still not always obvious how to write about it as a social phenomenon. Although academic interest in the Internet has quite rightly ceased to be confined simply to a specialized research niche, even today, a dissertation student whose fieldsite is online may be supervised by faculty who are experienced qualitative researchers but who do not write about the Internet themselves. Conversely, even a student born into this digital generation may need some help in working out just what aspects of the digital experience need to be explained for an academic audience and how to do so effectively. Both sides may know good qualitative writing about the Internet when they see it. Even so, deciding exactly how to make a piece of writing about the Internet compatible with the enduring principles of qualitative research, and formulating strategies to achieve this compatibility as effectively (and sometimes innovatively) as possible, can be frustrating all round.

Some very insightful general guides to academic writing and the challenges of qualitative writing in particular are available, and the annotated bibliography in Chapter 6 suggests some that I have found particularly helpful. It is true to say, however, that these guides often give advice that must be interpreted quite carefully before its application to Internet-derived data. Generalist texts on qualitative writing do not have to consider some of the very specific difficulties and opportunities that arise when fieldsites are online and data is born digital. This book was developed to complement those generalist texts, in order to distil some of the strategies that I have found useful in my own writing about the Internet and to pass on some of the features that I find impressive in the writing of others. I will not be duplicating the broader advice that generalists texts offer on how to structure various forms of writing, how to go about thematic or grounded coding of data, and how to get over writer's block (for these things are common to all qualitative researchers and covered well in the existing generalist texts). Instead, I hope to offer up some tactics that will help in deciding what kind of topics a qualitative Internet researcher should write about, how to introduce and contextualize online studies, and how to develop a purposive way of writing up qualitative Internet research for as broad an audience as possible.

I am thoroughly committed to the notion that the Internet is both a hugely significant social phenomenon of our time in itself and, in turn, a fascinating fieldsite for social science research of all kinds. Whether we analyze documents we find on the Internet, observe interactions that happen in online spaces, or carry out interviews via e-mail and instant messaging, we can be carrying out meaningful, mainstream qualitative research. By paying careful attention to the ways in which we write about qualitative Internet studies, it will often be possible to make insights based on Internet phenomena interesting and accessible, even for audiences who aren't interested in the fact that fieldwork is online per se. Qualitative writing about the Internet should be able to make broader contributions to sociology, psychology, anthropology, health research, media studies, and beyond, but achieving that will depend on judicious attention both to what is distinct from other forms of qualitative writing and what is shared with them.

An Arrival Story

Before moving on to discuss the kinds of contribution that Internet studies might make in broader fields of enquiry, I will first set the scene by explaining the personal interest that I have in qualitative research and in its application to the Internet in particular, and why I care about the way that we write. Ethnographies often begin with an *arrival story*, which describes the author's first encounter with the field and sets the scene for readers. This book is not in itself an ethnography (it discusses documentary analysis and interviews as well, although I do talk about a lot of ethnographies), but, all the same, I feel it would be useful to have an arrival story that lays out the territory and how I came to be involved in it because that explains the approach I take. My arrival at the writing of this text is a result of my interest in how qualitative research is written as much as it is a reflection of my interest in the Internet. My arrival story is thus also partly about arrival stories, as I will explain.

My interest in the question of how qualitative research should be written began when I was working in the Centre for Research into Innovation, Culture, and Technology at Brunel University in the 1990s, where I had been introduced by colleagues there to the sociology of scientific knowledge. I learned about perspectives in the sociology of scientific knowledge that had examined how knowledge claims in science are constructed. Pioneers in the sociology of scientific knowledge had argued that what appeared to be objective facts could instead be viewed as thoroughly social achievements (for example, Knorr-Cetina 1981; Latour & Woolgar 1986). It had become widely argued that scientific facts came to be accepted as such as part of a social process, rather than because of their inherent truth. As a part of this work, the sociology of science had examined some of the rhetorical tricks (or, more neutrally, "representational practices") that scientists used in producing factual accounts (Bazerman 1981; Yearley 1981; Lynch & Woolgar 1990). For example, the style of writing in the scientific paper (in which it appears as if the facts "emerge" on their own without the author being present, and in which writers are careful not to use the first person "I") was seen as important in establishing the objective existence of facts. It could, the sociologists of scientific knowledge argued, be otherwise. Scientific accounts could have been written in a much more personal, anecdotal style, but this would threaten our tendency to think of scientific facts as objective truths independent of any specific human intervention. The style of writing up research findings was therefore held to be highly consequential for making those findings seem robust, believable objects.

As a consequence of this focus on the style of scientific writing, some writers in the sociology of scientific knowledge saw themselves faced with a dilemma: should social scientists, having recognized those tricks, then deploy the same tricks themselves in making their own factual descriptions (Woolgar 1988)? If we accept the claim from the sociology of scientific knowledge that a particular style of writing within science helps a knowledge claim to seem more robust, should we use that same trick in our own writing? Or, does some kind of "epistemological correctness" prevent us from using it ourselves? Some authors in the sociology of scientific knowledge experimented with what happened to the knowledge claims of social science if the working of the rhetorical devices were exposed in the texts, or if new ways of presenting research were developed to avoid the more conventional tricks (Ashmore 1989). Debates ensued about the extent to which these deep forms of reflexivity diminished any chance the social sciences might have to make points that would be taken seriously in the world. I watched from the sidelines with some concerns about how I would ever find a voice for myself within this ethical and epistemological minefield.

At about the same time, within anthropology, attention was being turned to the construction of ethnographic research accounts, which traditionally were presented as if one ethnographer's experience counted as an adequate depiction of a whole culture. Clifford and Marcus (1986) crystallized a "representational crisis" in ethnography (Denzin 1997), focused around their recognition of the impossibility of an ethnographer ever writing a text that simply described a culture in the whole, as it actually was. Ethnographic writing, it was realized, could never be a straightforward portrayal of an externally existing world: it would always be subjective, selective, and, ultimately, a rhetorical construct, in many ways just like the scientific accounts examined by the sociologists of scientific knowledge. Ethnographers, too, have rhetorical tricks that are conventionally used to particular effect in their texts. For example, an ethnographic arrival story, as Pratt (1986) pointed out, does some useful rhetorical work in constructing the authority of the text: it helps to make the claims to knowledge that it advances convincing, as a product of the ethnographer's actual experiences. The arrival story tells how the ethnographer got into the field, but it also plays some crucial roles in establishing the identities of the key figures in the text—the ethnographer, the informants, and the readers. The arrival story lays out their relative positions and, crucially, it positions the ethnographer as the one who travelled to the far-off place and came back with the authority to tell readers how it was.

This initial interest in how ethnographic writing is constructed, and to what effect for the status of ethnographic knowledge, has continued and deepened over the years, delving into the consequences of particular styles for the "ethnographic self" (Coffey 1999) that we construct in the text. Other authors who have examined the rhetorical tactics and presentational styles of ethnography and provide stimulus for reflecting on the far from natural nature of qualitative writing include Van Maanen (1988), Atkinson (1990), and Wolf (1992). In each case, a further facet of writing that we might take as simply a natural way to express our thoughts becomes instead an artful construct that helps to naturalize some aspect of our relationship as observers and participants with the situations we describe and the audiences for those descriptions.

Taking on board the full implications of these observations on the rhetorical construction of knowledge risks steering us into a reflexive Mobius strip; there is no way out. For some, the argument is overindulgent, arriving too often at an epistemic or political dead end (Collins & Yearley 1992). For me, however, it stimulated a fascination with the mechanics of how we write to achieve particular effects. Even in academic fields where we are supposed to be writing factual accounts about how reality *is,* we are instead constructing that reality and bringing it into being with our words. To do so as qualitative researchers, we often use some of the same skills that fiction writers use to bring worlds alive on the page for our readers, even though we are accountable in different ways for the kind of textual worlds we create. Unlike some of the writers embroiled in the debates I described above, I did not feel moved to explore the alternative literary forms that attempted to do away with textual authority. Instead, I came away more aware of the responsibility that was placed upon an author when he or she claimed the right to say that something was so and with a concern to write texts that were crafted to reflect accurately what I wanted to say and no more (and also with a resolve to be more conscious of what it was that I wanted to say before I said it). The current text is born, to a considerable extent, of that interest in the mechanics of how knowledge claims are made in qualitative research in particular and a wish to make accounts that are properly responsible and accountable to their audiences and their informants.

A different kind of arrival story is necessary to account for my particular interest in the Internet as a site for research. My interest in doing qualitative research began with experiences of carrying out ethnographic studies within the sociology of science and technology. As a former scientist myself, I had moved into the sociology of science and taken up the practice of laboratory ethnography to explore how scientists adopted new technologies in their research, studying in particular what difference the increasing use of computers was making to laboratory-based science. In the 1990s, I found myself carrying out ethnographic studies of researchers engaged in genomics research, as they were making use of rapidly improving DNA sequencing technology, large databases of DNA sequence data, and various software packages available over the Internet to analyze and compare such data. Gradually, it seemed, before my eyes, much of the scientific work that had previously taken place in the laboratory seemed to be moving online. Online access to databases and packages developed alongside discussion forums for laboratory workers, mailing lists with announcements of events and resources, and a myriad of personal and institutional websites. New forms of collaboration and working together while apart emerged. Previously, I had subscribed unthinkingly to a mantra of face-to-face presence and bodily immersion in the fieldsite as the gold standard for ethnographic work. As my informants gradually spent more of their time online, engaged in work with absent others on a daily basis, it became harder to sustain a belief that face-to-face was best, and I found myself moved to grapple with the question of what part online experiences should play in ethnography. My initial interest in the Internet therefore arose as a continuation of the ethnography on which I had already embarked, as it seemed to be necessary to make sense of what the activity I was observing—genomics research—meant to those engaged in it.

This all took place in the early 1990s, and I therefore came to Internet research quite early in the mainstreaming of the Internet. From this initial interest in how genomics researchers were using the Internet as a component and extension of their laboratory work, I moved into various other projects, sustaining an interest in biologists using the Internet but also exploring in further projects how television and Internet intertwined in the realization of significant events and how new media came to allow for a different articulation of local communities with one another and with global projects. The situations have been very different, but the theme running throughout has been a focus on a rich and deep understanding of what use of the Internet means for those engaged in it (including what it means for me as an ethnographer). I have resisted and interrogated the urge to depict the Internet as a single phenomenon with monolithic implications, while attempting to disaggregate what it means for specific groups of people, under particular circumstances, in quite distinctive manifestations. Hopefully, in the chapters that follow, the broad question of "what are people up to when they are using the Internet?" will bring together the concerns of many of the readers of a book on writing qualitative Internet research. Precisely how that interest plays out will, however, differ quite radically for readers according to the needs of their particular projects.

Why Do Internet Research?

I have suggested that I came to the Internet by following a group of people who happened to begin using the Internet and that ethnographic instincts led me to follow them online. The extent of Internet use today makes it ever more likely that an ethnographer attempting to understand a group of people will, at some point, find them going online and will be tempted to follow. It is increasingly difficult for researchers attempting to gain the rich perspective on forms of contemporary life that qualitative research offers to ignore the Internet and other forms of mediated communication. Indeed, more research projects will start with the Internet as a site to observe in itself. However, despite an increasing tendency, at least in the densely connected countries of North America and Europe, to see the Internet as a ubiquitous and seamlessly linked part of everyday life, it is still often necessary to justify Internet research in academic circles. It may still be necessary within more traditional research domains, where face-to-face research remains the norm, to justify Internet research as something more than a niche interest focusing on a restricted and esoteric form of life. It is thus important to contextualize the Internet as a research field and to keep in mind those specificities of the Internet population that do limit its capacity to stand in as a straightforward reflection of everyday life offline. This must be done while also defending the nature of Internet communications as a form of living that is as valid as any other for the attention of the qualitative researcher.

The Internet is now a mainstream phenomenon in many parts of the world. The Oxford Internet Survey (Dutton, Helsper, & Gerber 2010) publishes figures every 2 years for the reach of the Internet within the U.K. population; for 2009, the headline figure was 70% of households and individuals over the age of 14 with Internet access, up from 58% in 2003. In the United States, in 2009, 74% of adults over the age of 18 and 93% of 12- to 17-year-olds were reported as having Internet access by the Pew Research Center's Pew Internet and American Life Project (Lenhart, Purcell, Smith, & Zickuhr 2010). International figures published by Internet World Statistics (http://www.internetworldstats.com) show that a significant digital divide persists between countries: their figures for 2010 have an Internet penetration of 10.9% in Africa and 21.5% in Asia, even though in absolute terms the number of the Chinese population online exceeds the number of Europeans online. Thus, although the internet is accessible by the majority of the population in many countries, there are also many parts of the world where those without Internet access considerably outnumber those who do have access. Clearly, we cannot research everyone, doing everything, online. The divide is not simply an international one, and more than just access is involved: some people are more likely to be in a position to make meaningful use of the Internet than others. Socioeconomic factors play a strong role in shaping access to the Internet, and some populations and some research questions simply cannot be accessed via the Internet. The implications of these variable rates of meaningful Internet access for the scope of Internet-based research findings are discussed in Chapter 3. For potential research populations without access to the Internet, qualitative researchers will continue to rely on other forms of presence.

Keeping in mind these caveats, as a mainstream phenomenon in many countries, the Internet has spread outside the very restricted segment of the population that it once inhabited, and it can now provide a means to interact with quite diverse social groupings. Certainly, for a social scientist wanting to find people who share a particular interest or fit the concerns of a specific research question, or to access a dispersed population within the confines of limited time and travel budgets, computer-mediated communication of some form has become an almost obvious choice. The headline figures on access to the Internet are, however, only a part of the story of challenge and opportunity for social science.

Simply saying that a lot of people have access to a medium does not, in itself, constitute a compelling reason to go there too (although it would seem increasingly perverse to ignore it). Possibly more compelling for qualitative social scientists as a motivation to go online is the sheer richness and diversity of what people do there. In the early days of the Internet, it seemed as though the Internet was going to be a rather limited way of communicating. The Reduced Social Cues model (Sproull & Kiesler 1986, 1992) predicted that text-based computer-mediated communication would offer an impoverished medium that might equalize participation, but at the potential cost of a lack of social feedback that would lead to disinhibition and reduced social order. However, despite these predictions, it rapidly became apparent that, provided with a means to communicate across distance, via text, with others whom they had never met face to face, many people did go on to form rich and lasting relationships and complex social formations. Howard Rheingold (1993) described the users of the WELL bulletin board system rediscovering a lost sense of community as they formed discussion groups around their interests and offered one another support, advice, and entertainment. Rheingold led the way in promoting a view of the Internet as a place where meaningful social interactions happened. In subsequent years, Steve Jones went on to forge a strong sociological claim for the Internet as a place where significant social activities happened through successive edited collections of papers focused on the notion of cybersociety (Jones 1995, 1997, 1998).

The richness and diversity of what people could do with the Internet was thus apparent even in its early days. People contributed to bulletin boards and newsgroups and developed their own websites. With the massive take-up of the participatory applications that have been popularly labeled as "Web 2.0" (O'Reilly 2005) and the increase in "user-generated content" as a core feature of the Internet experience, it has become even easier for people to add their own input to online forums and develop social networking activities. In tandem, the material of interest for social scientists has expanded beyond our abilities to make sense of it, such that some have declared that the Internet risks sidelining social research altogether through its capacity to distil and recombine information for anyone who is interested enough to explore it (Beer & Burrows 2007; Savage & Burrows 2007).

Analysis of online groups can be a means to research social issues that spill out far beyond the Internet itself. Increasingly, in their use of the Internet, people are simply going about their everyday lives. In the process, they leave traces that researchers across the social, psychological, and medical sciences have been able to draw on in tackling some fundamental issues. For example, Wen et al. (2011) describe a study of the use of online support groups by cancer patients, in which they tracked the use of the group by one woman on her trajectory from initial diagnosis through treatment and recurrence to her death. By situating their qualitative content analysis of the online messages in a context of disease progression, they were able to give a new perspective on the experiences of cancer patients and also to suggest new forms of intervention and support that professionals could offer to them.

The Internet is, to summarize, increasingly reflective of broad swathes of the population and of diverse activities: it is readily accessible, it allows for imaginative new research questions to be explored and for previously hard-to-reach populations to be accessed. It offers rich data on almost every imaginable aspect of existence. Internet research has developed from being a somewhat esoteric and unworldly frivolity to serving as a route to explore significant and weighty social issues. The opportunities that the Internet offers for social science are only just beginning to be realized. At the same time, however, we need to reserve some space for caution, and not just because of the (albeit very notable) risk that non-Internet-using populations will be further marginalized by lack of social science attention. Qualitative research on the Internet can seem as though it changes all of the rules, and it is important to remember that many established principles—not least the ethical duty of care toward research participants—still apply even when one is online. Qualitative Internet researchers make use of established frameworks, but often find themselves adapting them to take account of the distinctive social setting of Internet research. All writing needs to be attentive to readers, and, in the case of qualitative Internet research, we also need to think carefully about what the knowledge and preconceptions of our readership might be. Writing, for a qualitative researcher, is not just about reporting a set of findings. It is a process of crafting an intervention that brings out our experiences in dialogue with theoretical strands from our disciplines. It brings the concerns of the discipline into being as much as it brings the field into visibility.

The Opportunities and Challenges of Qualitative Internet Research

Through the Internet research projects I have been involved with, I have become very aware that the Internet, rather than being a monolithic phenomenon with singular effects, is instead a highly contextual phenomenon. My experience of the Internet will differ radically from another person's, as I navigate it in ways that make sense within my own circumstances. Other people's Internets will look and feel dramatically different to mine. Qualitative research gives us a really powerful way of exploring how that comes to be so and explaining the patterning of Internet experiences that emerges. Writing qualitative research is about taking rich and complex experiences and distilling them down into a more straightforward narrative. This is, however, inherently a thorny task for the epistemological reasons I described above, and it can often feel unsatisfying because of an awareness of the extent to which complexity is being left out or simplified. The Internet can accentuate this difficulty because of the colossal volume of data that can readily be made available for qualitative analysis. Archives of discussion groups or searches on websites can easily yield up a quantity of data that defies the ability of the qualitative researcher to attend to it in a meaningful way. The offer of plentiful data is made at the same time as the researcher becomes painfully aware of the pitifully limited stock of attention she can give to it. Of course, research in any setting can quickly overwhelm, but the availability of Internet archives and the ability to search data en masse accentuates the sense of the task's enormity in relation to the individual researcher's capacities. In the chapters that follow, I explore ways to address this concern through an ongoing reflection on the scope of research and the points that the writer ultimately wants to be able to make. This reflection is needed not just at the stage of writing up the qualitative Internet research but throughout the process of defining a study and generating data.

The proliferation of data is a general problem of qualitative research that is particularly accentuated in Internet settings because the researcher becomes particularly conscious of his selectivity in looking only at some data and not others. There have been ongoing discussions within ethnography more broadly about the artificiality of the notion of a fieldsite and the prospects for refreshing our notions of the field to incorporate recognition of diverse forms of location and connection (Marcus 1995; Gupta & Feguson 1997; Marcus 1998; Amit 1999). These issues relating to the identification of a research object take a very particular form in connection with the Internet, as it becomes moot whether online settings should be constituted as fieldsites in themselves or whether qualitative researchers should refuse to accept the online–offline boundary as a meaningful one to adhere to when designing studies. Qualitative researchers have always had to resort to pragmatic grounds for limiting their field studies, and it remains a question how far the online–offline boundary is defensible for bounding an object of study, whether that be for principled or pragmatic reasons. In the chapters that follow, mixed-site and mixed-methods studies will play a key role, and, even within an ostensive focus on qualitative Internet research, some of the studies that I discuss will have quantitative and/or offline components.

The Internet makes observable a broad array of social phenomena that have not been readily available to qualitative researchers before. As a diverse array of social activity has moved online, the "networked publics" (boyd 2008) that result have become accessible as researchable domains. Previously, the daunting social task of negotiating access to a segregated group in a way that is both ethically defensible and methodologically adequate had often been a barrier to the conduct of studies that researchers might have dreamed of exploring. Now, the extent to which otherwise "private" discussions go on in the public spaces of the Internet, and the persistence of many online interactions as searchable and archivable material, makes these previously impractical studies much more achievable. In ethical terms, then, are some studies now possible that we should still refrain from doing because they threaten privacy, well-being, or dignity? Many people discuss aspects of their lives online that they would not necessarily talk about comfortably face to face, either with their family and friends or with strangers. In online groups, the trust that develops through mutual disclosure over time, the disinhibition of anonymity among strangers, or a combination of the two can produce very frank styles of discussion. For social researchers, these developments expose to view aspects of social life that are otherwise very difficult to access. However, it cannot be assumed that covert research, just because it is more possible online, is necessarily ethically defensible. Circumstances often arise in which informed consent will need to be negotiated, either in securing consent to use a particular group as the focus of a study (as described in Chapter 2) or even after the event, in gaining permission to quote fragments of data in a research report (as discussed in Chapter 3).

In ethical terms, then, an online covert study is not necessarily any more justified than its face-to-face equivalent, and the Internet should not be treated as automatically available for social research without the consent of those studied. We also have to consider whether we would be able to rely on the findings of a study that simply observed online interactions without making any effort to involve the participants in the study and find out more about the contexts in which the online activities happen. In terms of methodological adequacy, is observing simply the online interactions sufficient for meaningful conclusions to be drawn? Can the study actually be reliable if it is not rounded out by pursuing its concerns more deeply into the lives of participants? Would we be able to trust what participants said about themselves? Put bluntly, can a study that only looks at online phenomena be more than mere voyeurism? As it happens, I do think there is a place for the online-only study because significant social phenomena that we might wish to write about do happen in online-only settings. However, this needs to be clearly justified throughout and positioned carefully within the resulting writing in order to make clear the point at which analysis becomes speculation and the design of the research object limits the potential conclusions. The ethical question persists throughout: simply because something happens online does not make it socially trivial or openly available as research data.

A further opportunity that the Internet offers for a qualitative writer is the chance to transform the writing process itself. The production of a conventional qualitative research text involves a retreat from the field; a period of reflection, aggregation, and assessment; and a time of solitary labor before a written text emerges. Inherent in this process is a period of separation from the field, in order to overlay the ethnographer's structure on the experience and allow her voice to come through in the final product. Although many attempts have been made at collaborative and participatory ethnography, and although large-scale qualitative projects may involve many researchers working together on joint analysis of field notes, interviews, and documents, the single-authored monograph, dissertation, or journal article remains the end product of many qualitative research projects. The involvement of participants in the production of the final text is often minimal, confined to invitations to comment on draft chapters. The same forms of online activity that qualitative Internet researchers are observing and participating in as field workers are, however, also open to them as authors. The Internet offers the possibility of expanding the process of writing the qualitative research text, more openly involving participants and other researchers, and producing writing that is more speculative, more ongoing, and less linked to a final monolithic text. Research blogs and hypertextual monographs offer the opportunity to render qualitative Internet research more open in format and to break down the boundaries between the production and consumption of research. As Chapter 4 discusses, the researcher may not necessarily decide to take up these opportunities (and many qualitative Internet research texts are written in traditional style), but reflecting on what blogs or hypertextual forms might offer is a useful way to consider, more broadly, the roles and relationships of writers and research participants and the forms of audience that we are embedding in our writing about the Internet.

Structure of the Book

Having used this chapter to establish a broad approach to qualitative writing as a skilled craft and the Internet as a valuable site to pursue the interests of qualitative research in contemporary life, I move on in the chapters that follow to explore in more detail just how we go about doing research on the Internet and writing about it. In Chapter 2, I focus on the writing that goes on in the research design process, discussing the writing of qualitative Internet research proposals, the flexible adaptation of research plans in the face of emergent online events, and the diverse forms of fieldsite that can result. The chapter discusses the role of theoretical concepts in shaping research. It also covers the agile practices of data collection and storage required of the online qualitative researcher, the different forms of online presence and interaction in which they might engage, and the ethical concerns that various forms of research design involving the Internet may raise.

Chapter 3 focuses on how qualitative Internet research methods can effectively be presented in research write-ups. Although, as Chapter 2 shows, the qualitative researcher will often be making situated judgments rather than following a preordained plan, the methods section of a research write-up needs to show how the decisions that were made helped to shape the resulting research in a suitable fashion. This chapter discusses the use of precedents to justify the researcher's decisions and explores the role of the methods section in establishing that data sufficiently rich to provide an in-depth understanding of a phenomenon have been collected. As part of this focus on how we bring our readers into the field, the chapter discusses the need for relevant Internet technologies to be described in an accessible way for readers, now and in the future. The chapter also looks at the ethical dilemmas that surround the presentation of data from qualitative Internet research, the interweaving of theory and data to demonstrate the broader significance of the research, and the opportunities offered by exploration of the temporal structure of the Internet.

Having covered the standard research report in Chapter 3, Chapter 4 then discusses some more innovative ways of interpreting data and depicting Internet research for print formats and for various new media. Making sense of Internet data brings challenges for qualitative researchers in terms of both the amount of data and the limits on its interpretation. These concerns sometimes prompt a turn to methods for preparing summaries and visualizations of complex data connections that blur the boundaries between qualitative and quantitative research. This chapter reviews some experiments in analyzing and presenting data in new ways, then moves on to new forms of writing. Qualitative Internet researchers have found that embracing Internet writing formats for the research itself offers up many new possibilities for presenting data and engaging research participants and readers in new ways. The chapter concludes with a review of those factors promoting and constraining a move to these new research formats.

The concluding chapter considers the current status of qualitative Internet research in sociology and explores its future prospects. A section on the evaluation of Internet research suggests a series of questions to ask of Internet research studies, focusing on criteria conventionally used in judging qualitative research. The chapter then concludes with a consideration of the future prospects for qualitative Internet research. Although there is considerable potential for further integration of qualitative Internet research with different forms of data synthesis and mining, and also an intriguing prospect of using Web 2.0 technologies more extensively within the research process to break down boundaries between production and consumption of research, there are also many challenges to be faced. In particular, the increasingly pervasive use of mobile and personal technologies seems very hard to integrate with the commitment of qualitative research to detailed and in-depth understanding. It is clear, however, that as qualitative researchers we cannot afford simply to ignore something that so many people do so much of, and, just as before, our methods and our writings will need to adapt.

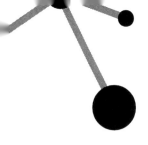

2

PLANNING FOR QUALITATIVE RESEARCH ON THE INTERNET

THIS CHAPTER focuses on how to write research proposals for qualitative Internet research. It discusses the necessary process of planning for this kind of research, while acknowledging that we will make changes to our plans as we go along. For a number of reasons, a proposal for qualitative research can be difficult to write (Sandelowski & Barroso 2003). Practical issues can easily get in the way of the research we would ideally like to do, as access to ideal sites can be hard to negotiate and the cooperation of key participants may be difficult to come by. Qualitative methods are also inherently adaptive, since we expect to change our strategies as we go along in response to what we find, rather than knowing in advance what will work for any situation. Indeed, the ethos of qualitative research involves the embodied researcher experiencing the world on its own terms and arriving at theoretical insights that are true to those experiences. Since the attraction of qualitative traditions is often precisely this appeal to a principle of allowing the field to speak for itself and being true to situations without imposing prefigured sets of questions upon them, a resistance to detailed planning can often be a source of actual pride.

Despite this focus on allowing for the agency of the field, however, the researcher must have something in mind in order to begin and in order to recognize a potentially interesting direction to pursue. The pioneering ethnographer Malinowski (1922/2003, 7) made a clear distinction between harmful "preconceived ideas" and helpful "foreshadowed problems" that a researcher might have in mind. An appropriate foreshadowed problem would be based on reading and reflection, giving the researcher an idea of what might be interesting and relevant to pursue once in the field. It would not, however, involve the researcher developing a rigid idea of what might be found or how precisely to go about finding it.

Qualitative research does, then, need to be planned, in that it needs to be a purposive activity conducted by a researcher working in a specific disciplinary context and in dialogue with a particular tradition. Researchers will often also have some idea of the beneficial effects that they would like their research to have, either in improving practice or enhancing reflection among practitioners in a given domain. Qualitative Internet research is rarely generalizable in a straightforward sense, but it will only be meaningful as a contribution to knowledge in so far as it can situate itself in relation to some broader set of interests or questions. A qualitative researcher might be looking to build theories and cast light on social processes or to provide rich descriptions of one setting to compare with another according to a set of theoretical propositions. Each qualitative study might be distinctive and unique, but it develops a dialogue with other studies through the theoretical concepts that it deploys. The researcher who wants to do useful research would do well to have at least some idea in mind at the outset of the broader concerns that his or her study might tap into or the comparative dimensions he or she might develop.

Moreover, in a contemporary climate increasingly concerned with value for money, with a solid evidence base for decisions, and with high completion rates for degree courses, and which therefore increasingly favors purposive research designs, we also have often to convince others of the potential worth of our research before we begin. Dissertation supervisors, funding bodies, ethical review panels, and sabbatical committees all need to be convinced that we have a clear plan, a realistic strategy, and a defined purpose that will bring back the required results. Under these circumstances, stating a principled stance on resistance to planning will rarely be sufficient to carry the day, and we will need to much more carefully identify at the outset how our research strategy is designed to meet our objectives and on what basis we will make changes as we go along.

In this sense, then, the writing of a piece of qualitative Internet research will often begin before the research itself has started, as part of a rhetoric of convincing others that the research is viable, ethical, and worthwhile. Qualitative Internet research in the contemporary climate must be designed, and this often involves preparing a detailed research proposal. It is important to be able to interrogate one's own proposed research design for its suitability to purpose because it will often be subject to interrogation by others before we have the chance to embark upon it. At the same time, however, our research designs still need to build in that principled flexibility at the heart of the qualitative research process that will allow the field to surprise us, to reorient our priorities, and to challenge our theories. The proposal will need to describe not just what we plan to do, but also on what basis we will change plans and adopt new tactics as we go along. The tension between the ethos of qualitative research and the contemporary focus on planning for results places a strong emphasis on developing a principled and explicit approach to situated decision-making, one oriented to maximizing the chances of the research for providing rich accounts of lived experience and theoretically meaningful patterns within that experience.

The final account of the research after fieldwork will often be very different from the proposal that we originally prepared. The differences are not present simply because as researchers we change our minds and encounter new situations as we go along, but also because the proposal and the research report are quite distinct forms of writing, aimed at different audiences and different rhetorical effects. Although the next chapter discusses a process of writing up the "cleaned up" account after the event, this chapter is about the research design process for qualitative research that we intend to do. Some overlap in content exists between the two forms of writing, but the style is different. In both chapters, I will discuss not just what to write about, but also how to present it effectively for the appropriate audience in each case. In this chapter, I examine key components of the qualitative Internet research proposal, looking at those research decisions that we make at the outset, at the theoretical background work that we need to lay out before the research begins, and at the activities that we plan for to generate the materials that will form the foundation for our subsequent qualitative writing about the Internet.

In the first section, I discuss the problem of choosing a fieldsite as both a practical and a principled decision that faces us at the beginning of a research project. In the case of Internet research, the concern that often faces us is whether studying online interactions in themselves will be sufficient for our purposes. I discuss some of the commonly occurring kinds of fieldsite that are found in qualitative Internet research, and I discuss the grounds for choosing among them. We also often have choices to make as to how we will interact with the people whom we study, and we will need to convince others that our chosen medium of communication with research participants is appropriate. Where online interactions, such as e-mail interviews, are concerned, our research proposals may have to face up to a prevailing skepticism about whether Internet communications are "real" enough for qualitative research. I explore some of the key concerns raised about use of online interactions with research participants and the possible counter-arguments we can advance. I also then explore some of the questions of access and ethics that have to be navigated before we can embark on our envisaged research projects.

Qualitative Internet research need not necessarily be about the Internet in itself, in that it can contribute to much more broadly framed questions about contemporary life. In the next section, I turn to the theoretical rationales for carrying out research on the Internet and discuss some recent examples of research that find something to say that readers who aren't necessarily interested in the Internet might want to hear. Finally, I turn to the practicalities of conducting research on the Internet, discussing the kind of skills the researcher will need to demonstrate and the orderly research practices of recording observations and cataloguing data that he or she will need to develop.

Together, these sections add up to the key components of a research proposal, encompassing where the researcher will go, how she will interact when she gets there, what the point of it all might be, and what skills will ensure that the research gets done. The form in which these are put together will vary depending on whether the research proposal is a bid for funding, a dissertation proposal, or a tender for a research contract. In each case, a key outcome of the writing should be that readers come away convinced that a specific piece of qualitative Internet research is the right approach for getting a defined and worthwhile job done. This chapter encompasses research designs involving documentary analysis, interviews, and ethnography, beginning with a set of issues most at the forefront of an ethnographer's mind—namely, identifying a fieldsite.

Fieldsites and Populations—Online or Hybrid?

Qualitative research, as discussed above, often takes pride in focusing on the experiences of the researcher in the field as the primary source of its insights. Ethnographers in particular are often counseled to resist any temptation to impose preformulated structures on their field of research. Instead, they are expected to develop research strategies and conceptual schemas grounded in the field itself, in conscious opposition to the predetermined stance inherent in many quantitative frameworks. This is not to say that qualitative and quantitative methods never go together, and there is indeed a healthy tradition of mixed-methods research developing (see, for example, Tashakkori 2006), but this too builds on the distinctive abilities of qualitative methods to add richness and depth and to interrogate taken-for-granted assumptions.

Although focusing primarily on qualitative methods throughout this book, in Chapter 4, I discuss further some ways in which qualitative and quantitative approaches can combine in the presentation of Internet research. In this chapter, however, I focus on the planning process for primarily qualitative approaches to the Internet. Particularly in this section, I focus on determining where the field is. If qualitative researchers want to allow the field to speak to them, how will they know when they are in the field and how will they recognize it when it speaks? This is a nontrivial question in an age of mediated communications that are thoroughly embedded in everyday life, in which a qualitative researcher can be sitting at his own desk and simultaneously be "in the field" via an Internet connection. Indeed, a qualitative Internet researcher need not be at a desk, but could be checking e-mails on the weekend or browsing websites via a mobile device while commuting home and yet still be present in the field.

This ability of the Internet to interweave itself into our lives, threatening the separation of "here" and "there" and making people and places appear accessible across distant times and spaces, troubles the notion of fieldwork and fieldsite. How will we know when we are properly there, and how can we tell when we've left? How will we know if we have found the right field for the research that we want to do? For qualitative researchers, indoctrinated with the idea that we need to be co-present with our research, it can be very troubling to contemplate a field that we can't define in advance, that we can't be sure whether we have effectively inhabited, and that we may find it very difficult to leave behind.

The traditional ethnographer of legend would be expected to travel to a place that she would define as her fieldsite because the people she were interested in lived there. The ethnographer would remain there for a period of time, participating in and observing everyday life, and using a variety of instruments (such as interviews, diaries, maps, and kinship charts) to assist her in documenting what she found, amassing materials for an in-depth and rounded understanding of that form of life. She would then come home from the field, leaving her research subjects behind, and indulge in a further period of reflection and interpretation that would lead to the writing of the final report.

This rather caricatured depiction of fieldwork depends on there being a recognizable place to go to that contains the people we are interested in. People, of course, very rarely confine their existence to predefined places nowadays, and ethnographers have had to grapple with that complexity (Burawoy 2000; Hannerz 2003; Kien 2009). Various forms of mobility, including commuting, tourism, and migration, mean that people are not predictably contained in places. Diverse forms of mediated communication also increasingly interconnect people, whether through mass media or interpersonal interactions. It is only when you actually begin to study what people do that you may find out what significance place has to them and how their experiences are organized across time and space by different media. It is, therefore, not possible to sustain very convincingly the idea of a self-contained fieldsite that we can define in advance; indeed, ethnographers even in more conventionally conceived field settings often follow people between sites and explore their mediated communications as much as their face-to-face interactions.

Fieldsite choices are thus difficult to specify in advance and the notion of a bounded fieldsite in itself is problematic, with the fieldsite always to some extent a fiction (Gupta & Feguson 1997). The multisited conceptualization of fieldwork described by Marcus (1995) aimed to face some of the arbitrariness of fieldsite choices head on, by offering us different ways to define a focus for ethnography apart from geographic place. Researchers were encouraged by Marcus not to limit themselves to going to one particular site, but instead to follow people, objects, and various forms of connection wherever these took them. Subsequently, multisited notions of fieldwork have acquired considerable currency, although the term also attracts criticism for, among other issues, continuing to embed a notion of sitedness (Falzon 2009); *connective ethnography* (Hine 2007) or *itinerant ethnography* (Schein 2002) can be more useful terms.

Even though it offered a different way to think about the focus of fieldwork, multisited fieldwork was still constrained by the ingenuity, energy, and resources of the researcher. Practical contingencies will always shape our studies and influence our ability to pursue particular interesting insights from place to place. Having a limited focus is not, though, something that we necessarily have to apologize for, as long as we have some awareness of the contingent decisions and exclusions we make. Choosing a fieldsite to focus upon (or making any other decision when defining our object of study) has a considerable pay-off in terms of conceptual development: having some relatively bounded way of defining the study helps the researcher to focus on understanding something in depth, even though that understanding may be partial and the boundaries may be arbitrary (Candea 2007). Internet researchers will thus still need to develop some idea of the object of study at the start in order to concentrate effort and to frame the understandings they develop. In the rest of this section, I explore some different ways of defining an object of study for fieldwork involving the Internet.

Among early Internet ethnographies, one of the solutions to this issue was to construe online environments as places that could act as fieldsites in their own right. When the Internet was just beginning to become a mainstream technology, the pioneering online ethnographer Nancy Baym (1995, 2000) studied a Usenet newsgroup[1] focused on discussion of a soap opera. She participated in the group, observed interactions, conducted online interviews and questionnaires, and carried out detailed analysis of social roles and hierarchies, shared values, and evolving practices. Although she was open to following up those situations in which members of the group met face-to-face or used other forms of communication, her primary focus as fieldsite was the discussion group itself.

Baym's study led the way in establishing that the Internet could be a fieldsite in its own right and that online interactions could be sufficient for rich and complex social formations to develop. Just as conventional ethnographers could choose a specific place as the focus for developing holistic understandings of cultural complexity, so too an online group could be an appropriate choice of site for an Internet ethnographer. This is not to say that all potential audiences for the research were convinced that online groups were an appropriate focus for ethnography, and the seeming neglect of real-life frames of reference that made online interactions meaningful remained a concern for many more traditionally oriented ethnographers. Nonetheless, the model of online ethnography had widespread appeal, and many studies of online fieldsites focused on discussion groups, websites, social networking sites, and virtual worlds followed.

Baym studied her group by focusing largely on their online interactions. This offered a rich site for her to develop a conceptualization of participants as involved in a community in three senses: as audience community, as online community, and as community of practice (Baym 2000). An online focus (with strategic forays into other settings) was, in this instance, appropriate for the study. Doing fieldwork online can be an immersive, intense, thoroughly engaged experience, far beyond simply reading words on a screen. For example, Lysloff (2003) argues that the study of an online music community was an appropriate choice for an ethnographic fieldsite and describes vividly the intensity of engagement that doing fieldwork in this setting involved.

However, such a focus on online interactions in themselves is not always going to be an appropriate choice, and, indeed, to define a study by the boundaries of a particular online environment will

---

1. Usenet newsgroups were asynchronous, text-based discussion forums each oriented to a specific topic, such as the soap opera that participants in Baym's (1995, 2000) study discussed.

often not be a decision that is culturally meaningful to participants themselves. Just as participants contextualize their actions in a particular online environment in relation to diverse frames of reference, so too will the qualitative researcher need to look in various places to work out how something that happens online makes sense to the people involved. Jones (2004, 21) observes that "Reading many academic accounts of computer-mediated communication, in fact, leaves one with the impression that such interaction takes place in a kind of virtual vacuum with little connection to the material worlds of the people sitting in front of computer screens and producing the words that analysts spend so much time dissecting and interpreting." If we want to understand those material worlds in any depth, we may need to go to them.

One study that made considerable efforts to contextualize online interactions was boyd's (2008) exploration of teenagers' use of social networking sites. boyd describes a networked fieldsite in which she "moved between mediated and unmediated spaces to observe and interview teens" (boyd 2008, 45). Her study took in online fieldwork in social networking sites themselves, offline interviews, and observation in less structured and less predictable environments where teenagers hang out. She encountered some ethical concerns, however, that led her not to pursue individual teenagers across contexts; instead, she chose to interact with them "one context at a time" (boyd 2008, 86). This was, then, a multisited study involving a hybrid of online and offline interactions, but not necessarily combining different forms of interaction with the same person.

Even studies focused on the Internet in itself will thus often not be conducted wholly online, or wholly within one online environment, since people do not live in online communities, or not exclusively at least. If you only look online, then some aspects of people's lives are going to be ignored or only available to you as hearsay (Paccagnella 1997). There is, on the other hand, an argument to be advanced about the authenticity of understanding that an ethnographer gains from experiencing the world as the people being studied experience it (Hine 2000). If we want to understand an online environment in which the people do only ever meet each other online, then the ethnographer needs to take the time to understand and reflect upon what that virtual-only knowledge of one another means for those concerned, rather than rushing off straight away to triangulate what they say online about their offline lives with face-to-face observation. We may, therefore, have to accept that not knowing all of the demographic details of informants, or not being able to pursue them into other aspects of their lives, is a part of the experience in which we are immersing ourselves rather than simply a lack for which the ethnographer has to apologize. Of course, this is a contextual issue to be evaluated in the light of a particular research question.

Face-to-face interactions, therefore, need not always be taken as the grounding context within which online interactions are framed. This kind of prioritization of face-to-face interaction cannot necessarily be justified a priori. It may well be a question to be explored in the course of the research itself: just what links online and offline together in a particular circumstance? Orgad (2005a, 63) describes online and offline as mutually contextualizing, and in her study of breast cancer survivors, she discovered that "reflecting on the move from online to offline endorses our thinking about the indeterminacy of the Internet and the complexity of the relationship between online and offline experiences." As Beaulieu (2010) describes, it is more important to focus on being co-present with participants, in whatever form presence takes for them at that point, than to be fixated on being co-located.

Clearly, then, the choice of a fieldsite (or other form of focus) for qualitative Internet research can be tricky and controversial. Both in the initial research proposal and in the final write-up, it will be necessary to specify how the fieldsite was chosen and to explore the conceptual limits that the choice of particular fieldsite boundaries imposes and the grounds upon which we might base a decision to change the focus and location of fieldwork along the way. Looking only online can be problematic in that it limits our ability to explore and account for the diversity of understandings of the Internet. Participating in a virtual environment may mean very different things to different people. Using a social networking site to keep up with your friends is very different, spatially and experientially, to immersing yourself in a virtual world and taking on a whole new identity. Both have some way of being meaningful activities for the people who indulge in them, but the frames of meaning-making drawn on may be very different. The choice of fieldsite for a qualitative researcher wanting to understand those frames of meaning-making may therefore also differ dramatically.

Although we often talk about the Internet as if there were a clear boundary between "real" and "virtual," in practice, often no clear cut distinction exists (Miller & Slater 2000). Marshall (2010, 12) refers to the "ongoing boundary ambiguities" that surround the Internet and the sites within it, such that what seems a quite discrete cultural site under some circumstances can also be seen as part of a complex of different intertwining communication practices that connect and mutually contextualize one another. Researchers have thus often been drawn to more itinerant ethnographic strategies to follow those cultural practices that pass through, but are not encompassed within, the Internet, such as Constable's (2003) study of "mail order brides" or Leander and McKim's (2003) study of the online activities of adolescents. Farnsworth and Austrin (2010) show how attempting to follow the research object "global poker" led them through a networked array of engagements that problematize any straightforward notion of a fieldsite.

There are, then, many different ways of designing and conducting a qualitative Internet study involving fieldwork. Boellstorff (2010) identifies three distinct approaches to ethnography of virtual worlds (such as the website Second Life). He suggests that the research can focus on a single virtual world in its own right as a fieldsite. Alternatively, the researcher can choose to explore connections between more than one virtual site (or form of online interaction), or he or she can focus on links between a given virtual world and the "actual" life of participants. Fieldsites will often be networks, involving strategic combinations of offline, online, and "imagined" spaces (Burrell 2009).

It stands to reason from this discussion that it will often not be possible to clearly define the scope of fieldwork in advance. Where the boundaries of online sites are ambiguous and the mutual contextualizations between different sets of practices fluid and unpredictable, we cannot know in advance where we will need to go in order to make sense of a phenomenon. Judging the boundaries of an online study can be highly complex, and, indeed, finally knowing what the fieldsite should have been can be the end point of a piece of research rather than something that could be known at its beginning. Itinerant and connective strategies place a lot of emphasis on making situated decisions about directions to pursue.

Despite this emergent quality of the field for an online qualitative study, it is still necessary for a proposal writer to attend to expectations that research should be focused and purposive. The proposal for this kind of qualitative Internet research will need to make a convincing case for an initial conceptualization of a field-site or form of fieldwork appropriate to the phenomenon being explored. It should be made clear that defined strategies exist for deciding which leads to follow up and which should be linked to the overall goals of the research in theoretical or conceptual terms. In this regard, it may help the proposal writer to reflect that, although each situation is unique, in any new setting there are likely to be similarities to other research designs. Citing precedents where other researchers have explored similar settings or faced similar issues helps the proposal reader to be convinced that the proposal writer is prepared to make sensible and defensible on-the-spot decisions.

As a starting point for strategic thinking about the shape that online fieldwork might take, here are some possible scenarios that link a research question to a fieldwork design (none is identical with a specific published study, but they draw in part upon the following works: Madge & O'Connor 2002; Gray, Klein, Noyce, Sesselberg, & Cantrill 2005; Taylor 2006; Drotner 2008; Beaulieu 2010; Wesch n.d.):

- *How do players of online multiplayer games maintain trust and reciprocity?* This question initially suggests an online-only study, focusing on one particular game (or comparing more than one game or guild within a game if resources allow). The research could focus on documenting a site-specific culture and its practices. Here, it would be appropriate to focus primarily on the online site, but the researcher would be alert to other communication channels habitually used by participants and would follow these to the extent that they appeared significant and relevant in supporting the culture being observed online. It is less relevant, for this specific research question, to know who the players actually are in their offline lives except in so far as this is something they know about each other.
- *Are online video-sharing sites democratizing access to media production?* Here, the researcher would want to become thoroughly familiar with a video-sharing site and would spend a lot of time in watching videos and reading

comments. However, he or she might also wish to produce his or her own videos in order to experience full participation in the culture. Finding out how video production was meaningful to participants probably would entail, at the very least, online interviews, but might well extend into offline observations, and a researcher might want to visit participants and study the making of videos first-hand.

• *What do online parenting discussion forums tell us about contemporary parenting?* Here, there could be a significant amount of online fieldwork, focusing on the site-specific culture and practices of an online discussion group used by the chosen population. This would, however, only give access to active participants in the group, and neglect lurkers.[2] It would probably be helpful to complement the study of active group members by looking also at how people who only read the group, without participating, make use of what they read. The study could usefully explore how people interpret the information that they gather from the group and what its significance is as a form of social support and supplement to other forms of expertise. This part of the research, again, would expand the fieldsite beyond the confines of the group itself and might well take the research offline.

• *Do teenagers use online health advice to supplement or replace other sources of expertise?* Here, it might well be helpful to begin offline, recruiting teenagers to interview about health advice in general and about their use of the Internet and also engaging them in "accompanied surfing," asking them to show the researcher how they might search for information and what they make of the sites they find. This could be complemented by an in-depth study of the forms of advice site aimed at teenagers, allowing the researcher to comprehend the extent to which personal searching practices and interpretations shape the experience of the web.

---

2. Lurkers are people who read a discussion forum without posting any messages themselves. It is very problematic both for other participants and for researchers to tell who they are and what they make of their reading of the forum.

- *How is contemporary scientific research carried out?* This very broad question offers up a wide choice of different starting points. We might start in a laboratory, watching what people do day by day, then gradually follow the products of their research as they travel out into the scientific publication process, are uploaded into databases, and presented at conferences. We might, instead, begin the research in an online discussion group and subsequently contact participants and visit them in their laboratories. Contemporary scientists can be very mobile across physical and virtual space, and, to capture this, a researcher would probably find himself needing to be mobile also, in order to understand the conventions of and connections between the different forms of space.

In each case, the scope of the fieldwork depends very much on what it is that the researcher decides that he or she wants to find out. Depending on the scope of the study that he or she eventually carries out, the researcher will end up knowing different things about the participants. It is important, then, to be able to write an initial proposal that justifies a strategy for defining fieldwork and convincingly claims to know in advance what might be relevant to explore the issue the researcher hopes to understand. As the research goes along, a deeper understanding of what the fieldsite should be, in terms of the contexts that the people involved use to make sense of what they do, is in itself one of the products of the research.

Online Presence and Effective Interaction

The previous section focused primarily on fieldwork and thus assumed an ethnographic approach to qualitative Internet research. Much of the qualitative research that has been conducted on Internet interactions has not, however, explicitly followed an ethnographic tradition. Rather than defining a fieldsite as such, many qualitative researchers begin by defining a population whose practices and culture they wish to understand. In this case, instead of adopting the holistic and often naturalistic norms of ethnographic research, such researchers may simply be looking for a means of finding out about their population of interest and exploring their perceptions of a particular issue. For these researchers, the concern with online interactions will often be that, although they offer a practical way to develop interactions with research participants, there are enduring questions about the adequacy of online interactions as a tool for qualitative research.

As outlined at the beginning of this chapter, qualitative research tends to pride itself on producing a rich insight into its focus of concern, developed without imposing preformulated concepts upon the situation. In an interview-based study, this concern translates into an attempt to develop circumstances under which the interviewee can speak in his or her own terms and use his or her own frames of understanding as naturally as possible, albeit within the inherently unnatural context of an interview setting. Qualitative research has thus embraced the open, narrative, and semi-structured interview, the life history, and the diary as alternatives to the structured format offered by a survey or questionnaire. The interviewing techniques that qualitative researchers learn are focused upon encouraging talk without imposing upon the interviewee particular ways of seeing the situation.

These techniques have become a naturalized part of the repertoire of research methods. A researcher proposing to carry out face-to-face interviews will rarely feel moved to explain the foundations of the interview method as an approach to exploring culture. Although an extensive methodological literature exists on the interview as a technology for constructing particular versions of the self (for example, Atkinson & Silverman 1997), such debates rarely feature in research proposals. Instead, the use of the face-to-face interview to access what people think is often taken for granted.

By contrast, online interactions can be shrouded with suspicions about their authenticity, and this concern means that qualitative Internet researchers often have to justify in some depth why online interactions are a good enough means to explore the experiences of the population of interest. This is particularly significant if the goal of the research is not to produce understanding of the Internet in itself, but is oriented instead toward using online methods as a research tool to explore a broader social issue. Where this is the case, the use of online interactions will need to be carefully justified as a means of finding out the relevant aspects of what people actually do, feel, and think (and, indeed, despite the wealth of erudite methodological debate about interviews mentioned above, much of the concern about online interviews seems to return to somewhat cruder concerns about whether people online are "really" who they say they are or whether they are just making it all up).

Some potential benefits of online interactions can be advanced in justifying an online interview strategy. It can be an advantage to offer people the time for reflection that an asynchronous online interview medium such as e-mail offers (Bampton & Cowton 2002). Where the topic is particularly sensitive, participants may value the time to compose themselves and come to the research topic when they feel ready for it, which e-mail offers (Illingworth 2001). Some characteristic of the research population may make a face-to-face interaction particularly difficult for them, and computer-mediated research settings can help them to feel comfortable in the interaction (Scott 2004); thus, online methods can form part of a more inclusive approach to qualitative research (Seymour 2001). An online interaction can be a useful way to rebalance power between research participants and researcher, although the resulting lack of control for the researcher over when, if ever, participants reply, can be immensely frustrating (James & Busher 2006). Although there may be a tendency for participants to be somewhat terse in their initial replies, particularly if presented with a lot of questions at once, this can often be overcome by techniques to reassure participants and encourage more extensive responses, including giving overt feedback, inviting open-ended storytelling, and using self-disclosure by the interviewer to develop reciprocity (Kivits 2005). Sometimes, it may be useful to encourage participation between participants in an online form of the focus group (Kenny 2005, Morgan & Lobe, 2011). Different forms of online interaction offer different benefits as interviewing tools and come with diverse challenges for the interviewer (McCoyd & Kerson 2006; Kazmer & Xie 2008).

Real-time interactions, such as chat and instant messaging, can be a natural medium for some populations (often younger participants, although this cannot be assumed in advance). Using a medium that participants find natural and transparent will be an enormous advantage for the qualitative researcher wanting people to relax into an interview situation. In that sense, the closer the fit between the medium chosen for the interview and the participants' everyday practices, the better, although the researcher too will have to be competent enough to carry the situation. This competence can have many facets, beyond simply being able to press the right buttons. During her ethnographic research in the game Star Wars Galaxies, Sveinsdottir (2008) spent considerable time "skilling up" so as to become adept enough to take part in interactions without hindering other players. She also developed an in-game social scientist character who could plausibly interview other participants in-character, to supplement her out-of-character online and offline interviews. In any online setting, an element of cultural competence will be required to use the technology effectively (so the researcher doesn't appear like an irritating newbie), to go along with the technical competences needed to interact at all.

To be convincing, a proposal for using online interactions to conduct qualitative research will need to justify why the chosen medium of interaction is appropriate for this particular population. Some background research will therefore often need to be done to establish that the chosen medium is an accessible and a comfortable one for this particular population and that the time constraints that a synchronous or asynchronous medium[3] imposes are appropriate both for that population and for the demands of the research topic. boyd (2008) discovered that pursuing people between media could be problematic in ethical terms, whereas Orgad (2005a, 2005b) found that some people were much more forthcoming in one medium than another. In designing qualitative Internet research, the researcher must reflect carefully on whether to combine interactions across media or stick to only one medium with each participant.

In determining the most likely comfortable communications media for a particular population, some very general statistics are likely to be helpful. The Pew Internet and American Life project (http://www.pewinternet.org/) conducts studies that highlight the very situated nature of Internet interactions and their diverse meanings among different social groups. The Oxford Internet Survey (http://microsites.oii.ox.ac.uk/oxis/) provides, for the

---

3. An asynchronous medium, like e-mail, allows a message to be sent at one time and read and responded to at another time. For synchronous communication, such as a chat room or online role-playing game, all parties to the interaction need to be online simultaneously.

United Kingdom, a twice-yearly snapshot of the state of Internet usage, looking at those sociodemographic variables that affect the use of various online media and other household information and communication technologies. Even such bald statistics as the country-level assessments carried by Internet World Statistics (http://www.internetworldstats.com/) can provide food for thought when thinking about who, globally speaking, might be excluded by research designs dependent on Internet media in general, although not down to the level of specific modes of communication.

These sociodemographic and national assessments of the usage of the Internet and various forms of communication can provide some starting points for thinking about whether one's chosen medium is at least accessible on a basic level to the people one wants to include. Beyond this, however, some pilot research, based on asking people what they do or observing their existing interactions, will probably be needed to get beyond the generalities of sociodemographic characteristics and into the communication practices of the culturally meaningful social groups that are most often the focus of qualitative research. It is, after all, no good assuring people that their sociodemographic characteristics mean they should be avid users of social networking sites if they are telling you that they have nothing to do with them.

Thus far, I have described active interaction with research participants. There is, however, a healthy tradition of unobtrusive methods that observe naturally occurring behavior without the researcher intervening with questions (Lee 2000), and use of the Internet can fit quite readily into that tradition. I have found that observing how people talk casually in online settings about television can be a very useful, unobtrusive method for media studies, using Internet search engines to look for passing mentions of a show outside of the intense fan engagement that occurs in dedicated discussion forums (Hine 2011). Seale et al. (2010) observe that the balance has shifted, so that observing naturally occurring interactions (via discussion forums) is actually now less labor-intensive than conducting interviews. He describes the discussion forum as a site where researchers can gain direct access to the way people discuss their health experiences as they happen, rather than the more formalized retrospective accounts that can be offered in interviews. Neither situation is to be taken as the foundational truth of how people experience health and illness, but each has strengths that can become part of the researcher's repertoire.

It can be helpful to use unobtrusive methods when the topic is sensitive or unlikely for people to discuss comfortably in face-to-face settings. Harvey and colleagues (2007) used qualitative and quantitative methods to explore a corpus of messages from online forums focused on the concerns of adolescents about sexual health. The researchers reflected that the online corpus revealed a frank and detailed discourse that contrasted strongly with the coy use of euphemisms more often encountered by researchers using traditional methods to explore the topic.

Archives of Internet discussions, blogs, and websites offer a rich array of data for the qualitative researcher looking for an unobtrusive method to capture naturally occurring responses, even though all of the previously mentioned caveats about lack of contextualization and knowing who people "really are" apply, as do concerns about the specific sociodemographic characteristics of those who actively use the Internet. It is also important to take into account the conventions of the site where the data are found and how these shape what people say, just as the conventions of an interview setting shape what people say. Nonetheless, an archive can offer an insight into the rich detail of everyday life, as amenable to a detailed discourse analytic inspection as it is to a large-scale quantitative exploration, such as Thelwall's (2008) study of contemporary swearing using data garnered from social networking sites.

Ready-to-hand tools, such as search engines, offer an easy way to locate material relating to a topic of interest. It is important, however, not to take the results offered by the search engine as a straightforward reflection of what is out there. Considerable amounts of material on the Internet may not yet have been indexed by search engines, and the ranking algorithms used by the search engine may shape the results list in ways that the researcher is unaware of (and cannot fully access, since ranking algorithms may be proprietary information) (Levene 2010). A Google search, for example, will contain an ordered list of results that look both comprehensive and meaningfully related to the topic, but use of a different search engine might produce a very different result. There may also be implicit sociopolitical judgments within search engine design that a researcher may not wish to adopt unquestioned (Harvey et al. 2007; Goldman 2008). Use of the Internet

as an unobtrusive method of observing society, and adoption of
a search engine as a means of accessing these observations, does,
therefore, have to be approached with some caution about the
extent to which it provides a straightforward mirror of society.

  For a qualitative researcher, then, the Internet offers a wide array
of resources both for interacting with participants and for unob-
trusively gathering observations. Decisions must be made about
how active the interaction with participants needs to be and which
medium will be most appropriate. Social and technical skills will
need to be honed for the medium. The research proposal will need
to make a convincing case for why this medium, for this group of
participants, was chosen and how far the data that can be gathered
will answer the research questions that motivate the work. Whether
the research involves active participation or a more hands-off analysis of archival material, the proposal will also need to address the
ethical status of the research, considering how the researcher will
act to protect the interest of participants in the research. Indeed, it
is because people take their online lives seriously that these online
lives become interesting for social research, so an ethical concern
becomes an almost inevitable consequence. Since establishing the
ethical standing of the research is often a key driver of detailed planning, this concern deserves a section to itself.

Access and Ethics

The ease of locating data on the Internet relating to practically
any topic of interest can open up research projects that could otherwise be near impossible, or where substantial work from an
experienced researcher would be needed to negotiate and sustain
access. The Internet has an immense potential to stimulate social
research by overcoming these barriers and making previously hid-
den or ephemeral aspects of social life accessible to the researcher's
gaze and persistent over time. However, when research objects are
manifested online, it can be easy to forget the niceties of negotiating access and to assume that anything one can access is fair game.
This is not how many people using the Internet—and inadvert-
ently generating what we see as "data"—would see it. Quite early
in the development of Internet research, it became clear that many
participants took their online lives very seriously and would resent
it if their words were to be appropriated without permission for

research purposes. Negotiating access for Internet research, and acquiring ethical approval to go ahead, have since become standard points of passage for online researchers.

The realization that, on the Internet, some projects could, practically speaking, be done, but ethically should not be done, can be a difficult one for qualitative researchers to cope with. Much of the dilemma revolves around the contrasts between what is publicly available on the Internet and what the people whose activities produced the data would perceive as being legitimately available for research purposes. As the Association of Internet Researchers recommendations on ethical decision-making for Internet research describe "online researchers may encounter conflicts between the requirements of research and its possible benefits, on the one hand, and human subjects' rights to and *expectations* of autonomy, privacy, informed consent, etc." (Ess and AoIR Ethics Working Committee 2002, 3). These Association of Internet Researchers guidelines for ethical conduct in online research offer up a set of questions for the researcher to ask him- or herself before proceeding with a research design, focusing not only on whether information is publicly available, technically speaking, but whether participants have expectations about its privacy that might be violated by the research.

In formulating a proposal for qualitative Internet research, it is important, then, to lay out the grounds for believing that data are both practically and ethically speaking available for research purposes. This information will be important for a funding body or dissertation committee to assess whether a viable project is being planned. It will be even more important when ethical clearance is required from an institutional review board or ethics committee. A review panel will want to be assured that due attention has been given to informed consent procedures, that privacy is not being unreasonably infringed upon, and that the costs and risks to participants are negligible and in proportion with the proposed benefits of the research. Within this environment, then, whatever the commitment to agile research methods and adaptive fieldwork strategies, a plan will need to be formulated that both clearly outlines what the researcher is doing and why, and tries to predict how any ethical issues that may arise will be dealt with.

It is unlikely that a single agreed-upon stance will emerge on whether Internet data in general are available to researchers, since the circumstances of its generation and use are so diverse. It is for this reason that the Association of Internet Researchers' guidelines (Ess & AoIR Ethics Working Committee 2002) were formulated as questions for researchers to ask, rather than as rules to follow. Researchers are urged to consider whether the site being studied is subject to any formal terms and conditions of use or privacy controls, whether participants are in any way vulnerable and thus at higher risk or incapable of giving informed consent, whether the topics under discussion are particularly sensitive, and whether the form of research being conducted is particularly intrusive.

Although a "human subjects" model of ethical decision-making has been widely applied to Internet research (for example Eysenbach & Till 2001; Flicker, Haans, & Skinner 2004; Hudson & Bruckman 2004; Johns, Chen, & Hall 2004; Hookway 2008), some persuasive arguments have been made that some forms of research do not fit readily into this model (Bassett & O'Riordan 2002). Large-scale research that anonymizes data or focuses on patterns of discourse (Herring 1996) has often been held to be exempt from human-subjects concerns, although this kind of research can fall foul of the terms and conditions of commercially owned sites (see, for example, recent concerns over the availability of Twitter data for research purposes [Gaffney, Gilbert & Pearce 2011]). When exemption from informed consent processes is being claimed, it will often be useful to cite precedents and to be aware that the impracticality of negotiating consent may not, in itself, be sufficient to gain a favorable ethical opinion (Hudson & Bruckman 2004). Different aspects of the research act may also pose different levels of intrusion to participants. Even in unobtrusive studies, in which the act of observation in itself is not deemed to be harmful, it may still be necessary to think about whether a research report should quote directly from respondents without their permission, as will be discussed in Chapter 3.

Many online studies will require informed consent processes to be considered at the planning stage and this will, in practice, often entail several stages in negotiating consent. There may well be gatekeepers whose consent is necessary to access a given population, whether they be the commercial owners of a site with a formal position on terms of access, the moderators of a discussion forum, or the organization responsible for a website. A promising research project can easily be derailed at this stage, so it is important to provide potential participants with a clear and honest statement of the research goals, ideally framed so as to make the wider significance of the project and the professional skills of the researcher readily apparent to an audience often understandably suspicious of motives. Although researchers may worry about the authenticity of online interactions, they sometimes fail to realize that their own identity may need to be established and verified before potential respondents will trust them (Sanders 2005). To this end, it is very helpful for researchers to have a visible web presence, ideally including professional credentials and even photographs, to establish trust.

After negotiating access with gatekeepers, it will still be necessary, in most cases where direct interaction with research participants is involved and even in some where only passive observation is planned, to go through some form of informed consent procedure with every participant involved in the research. In most cases, an electronic consent form will be sufficient, but where research participants are particularly vulnerable or are under-age, a printed form may be appropriate (see forms used by Leslie Regan Shade, reproduced in the Association of Internet Researchers ethical guidelines [Ess & AoIR Ethics Working Committee 2002]). In cases in which long-term participation and observation in an online environment is involved, it may be necessary to post periodic reminders about the presence of the researcher. Although our research instincts might be celebrating the relaxation of participants into natural behavior unaffected by the presence of the researcher, an ethical conscience might ask whether it is completely fair to capitalize on the ability to lurk in this way.

The stance on informed consent and the case for ethical clearance presented in a research proposal will be based on working creatively to find solutions for new circumstances that are recognizably continuous with precedents. Some reference to the wider principles on which the approach to informed consent is based will often be helpful. It will also be necessary to think creatively about changes that might occur in the research strategy and provide for meeting these new situations in a principled fashion. If a project has received ethical clearance, any substantial subsequent changes to the research protocol may require the researcher to go back and renegotiate approval. It is, therefore, very helpful in the initial application to anticipate change and proactively identify potential solutions.

Concepts and Theories

In negotiating access for an online study, it is often necessary to explain why one wants to do the research. This "why" question can be very hard to answer at the outset, when a qualitative researcher wants to keep as open a mind as possible. However, for the purposes of focusing our efforts in sensible directions, it will be important to have some idea of the potential significance of our research. Penrod (2003) suggests that one way round this dilemma for the qualitative researcher is to focus discussion on the gap in knowledge that the researcher aims to fill, rather than on the specific theoretical position that will be developed. The gap in knowledge will generally be more than just simply stating that there are facts that we do not know and will instead suggest a wider relevance for the research. This frame of relevance can be drawn quite widely indeed where Internet research is concerned. The research might be focusing on the Internet, and on what seems to be a new and unprecedented situation, but the research can still be positioned as a cumulative contribution to knowledge in dialogue with what has gone before. Otherwise, each new Internet application that comes along risks being studied as an isolated curiosity, without allowing us to reflect on how it fits in with other forms of human existence.

When developing a research proposal for a piece of qualitative Internet research, it will, therefore, often be appropriate to explore literature that has little, if anything, to do with the Internet. In understanding what is happening on the Internet, researchers have drawn creatively on concepts from sociology, psychology, linguistics, anthropology, the arts, and beyond. In each case, a creative leap is involved in finding a way to fit the existing concept with the new situation. Nardi (2010), for example, uses activity theory to look at play as an aesthetic experience, as a route into her ethnographic research on World of Warcraft. This conceptual framing was not, however, necessarily there when she first embarked on the research, and she describes her initial forays into gaming on the basis of a curiosity piqued by her students' descriptions of playing the game. Baym (2000) also describes the beginnings of her research as a displacement activity from her graduate studies, before she gradually realized that her displacement activity could be her field of graduate study and could allow her to explore different manifestations of community in the experience of television viewers online.

Research can often, therefore, begin with a quite practical or tentative interest in a field of practice as somehow interesting. For this initial pique of interest to become a mature enquiry of wider significance, it will be necessary to find conceptual connections with other fields. Many qualitative researchers in fields of practice such as health and social policy find themselves drawn into qualitative research by quite immediate problems that they face (Darlington & Scott 2002), but nonetheless need to broaden out the relevance of the research beyond a particular time and space. Developing a conceptual framing of the research (for example, moving from "how does this particular set of people in an online forum communicate about their disease" to "how does this forum compare with other situations where lay and expert knowledge coincide") helps both to widen the relevance of the research and enrich the resources that the researcher can use to interrogate the data generated.

In particular, it is often possible in Internet research to make comparisons and draw analogies with practice in quite different settings. Juxtaposing two very different things and observing the ways in which they are, after all, similar, can really help to feed the researcher's analytic imagination. Qualitative Internet researchers are often able to make creative links with fieldwork in settings far removed from online interactions. Nardi (2010) makes comparisons with fieldwork in Western Samoa and Papua New Guinea, as well as with activity theory and other ways of theorizing games. Boellstorff (2008) draws a link between his experiences of Second Life and former fieldwork in Indonesia. By keeping alive the possibility of conceptual and theoretical links between Internet fieldwork and other fields of human experience, these researchers see their fields in new lights and expand the potential significance of their research beyond a mere documentation of a contemporary curiosity.

It should be possible, then, for qualitative Internet research to build cumulatively upon the foundation of disciplines from pre-Internet days and to find new ways to interrogate and illuminate existing concepts. By offering up a different form of human existence, the Internet can help to bring to light hitherto invisible assumptions about those other situations. As Markham describes, the Internet can act as a reflexive tool for evaluating our preconceptions "The intriguing thing about CMC [computer-mediated communication] is that it calls attention to ways we literally see and make sense of the world and points out many of the biases inherent in our traditional ways of seeing and knowing" (Markham 2005, 796).

In writing a proposal for qualitative Internet research, it is, then, important to reflect on what the research might have to say and how far this is something that readers who aren't already interested in the Internet might want to hear. I would suggest that a good rule of thumb is to examine the list of references drawn on in your research proposal and to worry if all of your references are to Internet research—or, indeed, if they all date from the advent of the Internet. The Internet can seem radically different from other forms of social interaction, but, even so, this difference should be established in dialogue with concepts already in currency in the cognate disciplines, rather than being assumed a priori. A convincing research proposal will lay out the grounds for a potential theoretical contribution that situates the Internet as a legitimate concern for a researcher within a specific disciplinary field.

To arrive at a preliminary conceptual framing of the research topic, it may be helpful to draw a spider diagram with the topic as you currently understand it at the center and connections to as many theoretical concepts as you can brainstorm around the edges. Figure 2.1 shows this type of diagram, drawn to depict one of my own ongoing research interests, the local mailings lists that many people now use to give away their unwanted items. This topic connects very clearly with various aspects of alternative consumption and also environmentalism and sustainability, but it also raised for me an interest in how people negotiate transactions and manage their security as relationships move from purely online encounters to face-to-face meetings at someone's home to complete the transaction. This kind of diagram can be used to help you to reflect on where your main interests lie: in my own case, my interests were more strongly drawn toward the move from online to offline relationships than to the environmental aspects. Having identified some tentative fields of connection, a lot of reading will also help, looking creatively beyond the narrow confines of searches for literature that exactly reproduces your existing

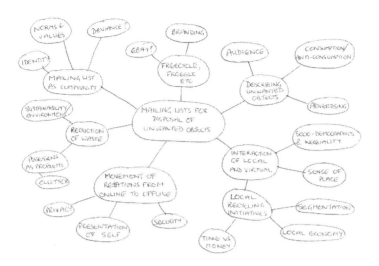

Figure 2.1 Spider diagram showing various conceptual themes connected with my research interest in locally focused mailing lists such as Freecycle and Freegle, popularly used to find new homes for unwanted objects.

research focus to explore different ways of seeing your setting. It helps to make reading widely and imaginatively part of the writing process, as this can become a way of making sure that qualitative writing about the Internet speaks beyond a narrow set of confines and connects us with our disciplines.

Research is often also intended to have some practical pay-off. Many of us hope, in some way, to be doing research that, even if not directly oriented to a practical goal, might help in informing someone better about their situation or enhancing reflection on a particular set of circumstances. Again, this hopeful intention to do useful research can come up against difficulties at the planning stage when placed against the openness and design-aversion of the qualitative stance. We are unlikely to be designing research that will have a predictable outcome, and what we can say about the use of the final product will always be hedged with caveats. At the proposal stage, it will, however, be appropriate to discuss potential audiences for the research that can be identified and to reflect on how their involvement might be secured, either during the progress of the research or by appropriate presentation of reports.

Fieldnotes, Transcripts, Screenshots

A convincing proposal for qualitative Internet research has a lot to do in persuading its audiences that the methods are appropriate and ethical and the goals suitably engaged in contemporary scholarship. An aspect often missed out, however, is establishing how the researcher will, practically speaking, go about doing the research. As qualitative research is a very engaged form of research, often involving the researcher using his or her own presence and communicative resources as the instrument of the research, it is important to establish how the research will be done, on a detailed blow-by-blow basis.

This is not to suggest that a qualitative researcher must always be perfectly prepared and up to anything. In a face-to-face research setting, researchers can and do make mistakes, upset people, miss important events, and fail to keep the right fieldnotes and recordings. Using your own presence as a research tool involves embracing that potential for fallibility and working with it. We are all to some extent making it up as we go along and getting by as best we can. However, the online setting offers up some particular challenges in the new skills that it requires, in the format and sheer quantity of data that it can generate, and in the need to embrace the particular qualities of digital data in terms of searchability, replicability, and sortability. As Garcia et al. (2009) describe, moving fieldwork online can pose significant demands on ethnographers to change their practices, and they will need to develop ways to engage with the full gamut of online experiences that a particular environment offers.

In a research proposal, one will rarely have space to give copious descriptions of how data will be stored. It is useful, however, to have some idea in advance of the forms of data that may be generated and the specific tools that might be needed to capture them effectively. A researcher in a face-to-face setting might rely on an audio-recorder and a camera, together with apparatus for taking notes. In an online setting, it may be necessary to provide oneself with software for downloading offline versions of websites of interest, a means of taking screenshots and movies of online experiences, together with ways of archiving blog[4] and micro-

---

4. A blog is akin to an online diary, usually focused around one person's time-stamped contributions interspersed with comments from readers.

blog[5] posts and preserving videos and podcasts.[6] Murthy (2011) describes a combination of technologies, including an Apple iTouch and digital camera with photo-sharing and blogging software, which he uses to create and share multimodal fieldnotes. Often, the needs of a researcher will go beyond the facilities that sites such as YouTube,[7] Twitter,[8] and Facebook[9] offer to their ordinary users, and third-party software will be needed. Although any specific suggestions I could make here would probably be out-of-date by the time readers are looking for their own solutions, it is comforting to note that such tools are constantly being developed, and researchers generally are happy to share tips about what works for them via discussion groups, such as the Association of Internet Researchers mailing list (http://aoir.org).

Online fieldwork and real-time online interviews can make considerable demands on the skills of the researcher to keep up with the interaction, focus on the participant, keep the goals of the research in mind, and make sure that the resulting data are being recorded. Depending on the setting, it may be necessary to keep up with fast-moving action in more than one medium at once, possibly following a text-based chat channel and an audio channel while trying to stay alive in an online gaming situation and still keep research thoughts in mind. An organized approach to naming files and storing information about people encountered online can be a great help here, as Guimarães (2005) discusses. When research is going to include a face-to-face component to go alongside online fieldwork, it is important to think about the extent to which the researcher will need Internet access in the face-to-face settings and to prepare for the additional demands

---

5. A micro-blog, such as Twitter, allows users to send short messages that are broadcast to their subscribers (followers).

6. A podcast is a prerecorded audio file available for download from a website.

7. YouTube is a highly successful video-sharing site, allowing users to upload videos, view them, and leave comments.

8. Twitter is a highly successful micro-blogging site that has featured in high-profile cases of privacy infringement and the circumvention of restrictions on reporting in the mainstream media, in addition to being implicated in the organization of new social movements and civil unrest.

9. Facebook is a social networking site that allows users to create personal profiles, upload photographs and other personal material, and communicate with their acquaintances.

that traveling and switching between computers place upon the storage and organization of research materials.

For research based on Internet archives, it can be tempting to allow the archive to do the work and not download the dataset to be stored under the researchers' control. Although some commercial sites may place limits on wholesale downloads of data, it can be very risky to rely on the continued availability of an online dataset, particularly in a long-term project. Similarly, it can be dangerous to assume that a particular online service used for interacting with participants will continue to be available for the duration of a project. I have had the disconcerting experience of organizing a series of chat room seminars with a group of my students only to have the third-party chat site we were using disappear without trace part way through the series. I had a committed group of students, and we quickly found another site to host our seminars, but if this had been a research project, I could easily have lost a large number of hard-won participants when the chat service failed. I learned the hard way that it is always useful to have a contingency plan and another channel of communication ready in mind when your research relies on any third-party service or software.

Putting It All Together: A Convincing Proposal for Qualitative Internet Research

Proposal writing is a form of writing unlike any other, with some discursive tricks all of its own. The proposed work must be conjured up with an aura of certainty, a promise to deliver, and a consciousness of the impending significance of its findings. At the same time, the researcher is aware of the contingencies of the research process, the need to adapt strategies as the work goes along, and the sheer scale of what is unknown and cannot be foreseen at the outset. Although, to some extent, a work of carefully crafted (albeit sincere) fiction, a plausible proposal makes clear that the researcher can at least design one coherent, significant, and doable study. Whether that is, in its entirety, the study that they actually go on to carry out is another matter.

The proposal for a piece of qualitative Internet research will need, I have argued, to address some concerns that are general to any piece of research, some that are more specific to qualitative research, and some that are quite directly related to the use of the Internet as fieldsite or medium of interaction with participants. The components of a convincing proposal will be arranged very differently, depending on the body that is to assess it. However, the following components are likely to need to be addressed at some point:

- What is the significance of the research? What practical issues does it address? What theoretical or conceptual work does it build upon and contribute to? Does it have an ambition to contribute to the development of a discipline beyond Internet research in itself?
- What is the fieldsite (or other defining object) of the research? Is the focus to be purely online, or are offline interactions also going to form a part of the research? Under what circumstances will the research move to another online environment or to offline settings? What limits does the choice of fieldsite or definition of object place on the ability of the research to inform development of theory or practice? How do these choices limit the reliability or generalizability of the findings?
- How will the research population be identified, and how will any interviewees be recruited? Will it be sufficient to appeal for participants via online forums, or will it be necessary, as is often the case, to develop a more personalized form of approach? What biases might this research population exhibit? How will the researcher describe the goal of the research to participants and establish his or her own credentials?
- How will the researcher interact with participants? What informs this choice of medium, and how does it fit with what is already known about the research participants? What steps will be taken to ensure that the resulting data have adequate richness and authenticity for qualitative analysis?
- How have ethical issues been addressed in the design of the research, and how will any unforeseen issues that arise as the research goes on be dealt with?

- How, practically speaking, will research materials be collected, archived, and indexed? What skills will the researcher need to acquire, and what technical back-up will be needed?

Depending on the intended audience, a research proposal in qualitative Internet research may need to make judicious use of citations to precedents in published research, in order to demonstrate that the approach is tried and tested and that many of the arguments have now become well rehearsed. The concerns of each audience will differ: a funding body may need more convincing of overall significance of the research to a wider problem, whereas an ethical review body may proceed very cautiously in the face of ethical dilemmas not previously encountered. With luck and careful use of rhetoric, covering the points laid out here, the proposal will hopefully be successful, the research will go ahead, and the researcher can progress to the stage described in the next chapter, focusing on writing the qualitative Internet research report.

3

REPORTING ON QUALITATIVE INTERNET RESEARCH

HAVING DISCUSSED in the previous chapter how we write proposals for qualitative Internet research, this chapter turns to the writing that we do after completing the fieldwork. Here, I will explore the quite different writing style that is needed when we report on our experiences, in order to present them in an evocative way and to interweave observations with theory. Whether the research is being written up for a dissertation, a journal article, a monograph, or a report for funder or sponsor, some constraints often will be placed on the format that we use. Different audiences have their own expectations about how research writing should be structured, and their guidelines will need to be followed. Alongside these formal guidelines (often broadly drawn to include any kind of research), however, there are some more specific stylistic conventions for qualitative writing that it is useful to know about. This chapter, therefore, moves between observations about aspects of writing quite peculiar to qualitative Internet research and discussion of the ways that broader stylistic conventions of research writing apply to writing about the Internet.

Qualitative fieldwork can be an intense, enthralling experience. When it goes well, it combines a pleasurable relief that people are saying the kind of things your foreshadowed problems led you to hope they would, together with an excitement about new aspects you hadn't anticipated unfolding before your eyes. The challenge of putting yourself into the research setting, adapting to it as you go along, trying to get by and to get the best from your experiences, can be a real buzz, partly because it goes along with the risks of getting things wrong, missing the best insights, or making a fool of oneself. One of the ways that I knew online fieldwork really was fieldwork was because I felt all of those emotions, even though I was still sitting at a desk in my office and the field was behind the screen. Online fieldwork still felt risky, exposed, unpredictable, and exhilarating.

In the midst of all of that adrenaline, despite the best efforts to write insightful fieldnotes on emerging themes and connections, it can be difficult to develop a coherent sense of the overall situation while actually immersed in it. Often, it is only after withdrawing from fieldwork, with a mass of notes, images, recordings, e-mails, archived postings, and screenshots, that it is possible to begin to develop a more orderly sense of what the cumulative picture that emerged might be. The process of writing up qualitative research involves something much more active than simply reporting on what we did. It involves finding a tale to tell and finding a way to say it that remains true to those intense experiences while at the same time presenting itself as a contribution to our understanding in a disciplinary context or field of policy application.

Writing up an interview-based study is also much more than simply recounting what was said in the interviews. When conducting an interview-based study, we often allow the experience of one interview to shape the way that we conduct the next. New themes surface to be followed up and emergent hunches are tested out. It is the strength of the qualitative in-depth interview that we allow the questioning to unfold, rather than asking the same set of questions each time. Even with this evolving, inquiry-led structure to the interviews, however, it will still usually be difficult to be clear about what it is that the research has to say until after the interview transcripts are all complete. It is in the process of reviewing the full set of interviews, coding and exploring emergent themes, and juxtaposing interviews against one another in systematic fashion that an overall sense of the story to be told emerges. Again, writing up qualitative interviews is an active process that creates a narrative far exceeding a simple account of "what people said."

Good qualitative writing is evocative of the field, but also theoretically informative. It has also to combine a precise approach to description that tells readers what we did, how, where, and when, with a creative flair that helps readers to feel that they understand how the situation that we are describing makes sense to those involved. One of the greatest contributions that qualitative writing makes is in displaying how forms of experience that might seem quite different can, instead, be seen as related. Theoretical concepts that transcend the specificity of any single situation are powerful tools that help us to render connections between diverse aspects of human experience. At the same time, good qualitative writing pushes our theories forward, questioning assumptions, developing concepts, and refining definitions.

One example of qualitative writing about the Internet that, for me, exemplifies this focus of qualitative writing on something other than the specificities of the situation is Miller and Slater's (2000) discussion of the Internet in Trinidad. They develop a set of concepts that are thoroughly rooted in their observations, but broad enough to invite comparative studies and encourage other researchers to test their applicability to their own situations. They write:

> In investigating the embedding of the Internet in a particular place, and vice versa, we are concerned with:
>
> *Dynamics of objectification*: how do people engage with the Internet as an instance of material culture through which they are caught up in processes of identification?
>
> *Dynamics of mediation*: how do people engage with new media *as media*: how do people come to understand, frame and make use of features, potentialities, dangers and metaphors that they perceive in these new media?
>
> *Dynamics of normative freedom*: how do people engage with the dialectics of freedom and its normative forms as they are opened up by Internet media?
>
> *Dynamics of positioning*: how do people engage with the ways in which Internet media position them within networks that transcend their immediate location, and that comprise the mingled flows of cultural, political, financial and economic resources? Miller and Slater (2000, 9)

These "dynamics" provide a frame for organizing the evocative descriptions that follow and offer up a resource for future researchers to explore as they relate to their own experiences. "Writing up" therefore becomes a very significant and active part of the process. We don't simply write what we did, but we craft our final written words on the basis of patterns that emerge as the process unfolds. We clean up our experiences to tell a tale that has a point to make for our readers: as Wolf describes it, "as ethnographers, our job is not simply to pass on the disorderly complexity of culture, but also to try to hypothesize about apparent consistencies, to lay out our best guesses without hiding the contradictions and the inconsistency" (Wolf 1992, 129). In any form of qualitative research, we have a duty as writers to do something more than simply place our material in front of the reader. We have actively to narrate it for them and to offer them a route through it (even though, as I will discuss in Chapter 4, new media forms can offer qualitative researchers some creative ways to deviate from linear narrative).

Wolf (1992) indicates a field of tensions that the qualitative researcher inhabits. Faced with a mass of research materials and the need to make some sense of them in a report, it is all too easy to veer the other way and present them as if the world were neatly patterned into themes. As Law (2004) points out, the world can be a complicated and messy place, and we can do it an injustice if we present too orderly an account of it. Too "cleaned-up" an account of patterns observed in the world also risks obscuring the extent to which our experiences, even as professional qualitative researchers, are subjective. From the influence of the interviewer's identity on the research to the effects of the ethnographer's presence on the setting and the role of our preconceptions in shaping what we see as data and what we make of it, qualitative researchers have been very aware that their accounts are not to be seen as objective truths. To present them as such would be in bad faith, and writing styles have adapted over the years to give contingency—and the possibility of alternative interpretations—a more visible presence in the text.

One way of fending off the risk of cleaning up reality too much is to give the research materials a strong presence in the text, offering the opportunity for readers to challenge our interpretations or develop their own alongside ours. In addition, a key aspect of qualitative writing that keeps the contingency of our interpretations open is the researcher's visible presence in the text. Although in much scientific writing the author is absent, use of the first person banned, and facts seem to emerge on their own without the agency of any human being required, qualitative writing tends to acknowledge the role of the author in the research and in the construction of the text. We use our embodied experiences as the basis of our writing, but, at the same time, we reflect on their uniqueness *as* embodied experiences. In the case of Internet research, this reflexivity can be very important in thinking about how our own prior experiences and current circumstances shape the Internet use that brings us to the research setting.

Some very useful discussions of ethnographic and qualitative writing styles can apply to any setting, including qualitative Internet research. Van Maanen's (1988) classic text on ethnographic writing styles remains relevant whatever the setting, and traces of the styles that he describes can be found in much of the recent qualitative writing about the Internet. Atkinson (1990) offers a careful exposition of the textual devices that ethnographers use in their accounts, while Goodall (2000), in more pedagogic style, discusses the processes of writing and interpretation, and, in his more recent (2008) text, explores the role of personal narrative. Silverman (2006) explores the process of writing up interview material, and Coffey and Atkinson (1996) discuss how researchers make sense out of qualitative data. Several of these texts predate the widespread use of the Internet in qualitative research, but their observations on styles of writing and processes of making sense of data remain highly relevant.

This chapter assumes that readers will have some background in qualitative analysis and explores writing styles in the specific context of qualitative Internet research. In the next chapter, I will explore different forms of presentation, including more creative uses of new media in research reports and some possibilities for visual presentation of data and qualitative-quantitative mixes. In this chapter, the focus is on a fairly conventional form of linear qualitative writing, of the kind that we produce for a monograph, report, journal article, dissertation, or thesis. The first section of this chapter discusses the methods section of the research report, outlining those factors that readers need to be made aware of in order to set our research findings in context. In particular, I discuss the concern that writing about specific Internet contexts has to be made accessible to readers who may not ever have encountered that particular application.

Following the discussion of methods, the chapter then moves to discuss the core of the research report, focusing on styles of writing that interweave theory and data and develop an evocative account of the field. I then explore concerns about anonymity and confidentiality that this richly data-focused style of writing about the Internet raises. After this, I explore the question of reflexivity and the very specific role that it plays in qualitative writing about the Internet. Next, I consider the temporal dimension of Internet research and look at the ways in which the timing of events features in qualitative Internet writing. The final summary provides a checklist of aspects to reflect on when developing a style for a research report.

Methods: Richness, Adequacy, and Limitations

A scientific research report has a standard format that many children learn in school science lessons, as follows:

- *Introduction.* Sets the scene for why the research was done, explaining the research question and drawing on relevant literature to set the scene. In a scientific report, the hypothesis to be explored in the research is stated here.
- *Methods and materials.* Discusses exactly how the research was done, in a detail that should allow another researcher to reproduce the study
- *Results.* Sets out the data recorded, including the outcome of any relevant statistical tests, and offers graphs and tables to allow data to be seen in full
- *Discussion.* Explores the interpretation of the results, setting them in the context of previous research and highlighting their significance in relation to the hypothesis

Qualitative research reports tend to have a freer approach to format, but in fact contain many similar elements. The "introduction" for qualitative research often contains an extended literature review that introduces prior work in the substantive field of interest and also lays out the theoretical concepts that the research draws upon

and contributes to. Instead of a hypothesis to be tested, w
an open, exploratory, but theoretically grounded research
appropriate for exploration by qualitative means. The separai
between "results" and "discussion" is often not as clear-cut as in
the scientific report, and, as described in the later sections of this
chapter, qualitative researchers often want to interweave theory
and data more creatively to develop a convincing and evocative
account of their fieldwork. However, some clear continuities exist
between the different styles of research writing, and one of these
focuses on the discussion of methods that allows readers to know
exactly what we did. Although a qualitative research report might
be a highly creative, personal account that deviates strongly from
scientific reporting style, still, by the end, our readers should know
clearly what it is that our account is based upon. Readers should
be able to contextualize our account as being about something in
particular and to understand its limitations based on a clear idea
of what we did and didn't do.

The "methods" section of a research report lays out with some
precision what the author did. All qualitative research has a specificity to it, and, given that the researcher is the research instrument, readers need to know who we are, what was done, and how
choices were made. For qualitative Internet research, many layers of selectivity shape the generalizability of our findings. To lay
the groundwork for a research report, it is worth being quite systematic about exploring what those layers of selectivity are. Some
aspects of the selectivity that we may need to write about are:

- *Who am I?* Since qualitative research depends so much
  on the embodied experience of the researcher, and since
  reflexive input may, as described later in this chapter,
  play a key role in reporting on the research, it can be very
  important to introduce ourselves. Relevant aspects of
  Internet experience and personal biography may need to
  be discussed, in so far as they shape our online interactions and our interpretations. This discussion should stay
  short of a full biography, which could become over-
  lengthy and unnecessarily indulgent, but should involve
  careful reflection on what it is about us that shaped our
  study and how, for someone else, it might have been
  otherwise.

- *Who are they?* A qualitative study will usually not focus on a representative sample of a given population. Instead, we develop a focus for research based on identifying a particular fieldsite or a group of people, both because we can negotiate access and because a theoretical or practical interest is piqued by them. Who those people happen to be shapes our findings, and, in qualitative research, we tend to present ourselves as having produced a rich account of how a particular set of people think or act, rather than a free-floating discussion of how people, in general, act. We need therefore to discuss the criteria we used to identify participants and the various forms of bias that may have shaped who chose to take part. Although we cannot be certain about some of the sources of bias, the researcher does have some responsibility to speculate on how far circumstances might have been different with a different set of participants. This is particularly significant if the goal of our research is not just to describe an Internet setting in its own right, but to use qualitative research via the Internet to illuminate some wider social phenomenon. We need to reflect on the various forms of selectivity that result from who uses the Internet in theory, who uses it in practice, who uses different Internet environments, and whose use is actually visible to the researcher. It is probably a highly selective portion of the population who are actually ever visible as participants in archived online discussions, for example.
- *What technologies did I use?* The technological focus of the research is particularly important and often tricky to describe in qualitative Internet research. As technologies evolve quickly, as niche interests develop in particular sites, and as popular applications change frequently, we cannot assume that readers will know what the technical platform that we used looks like. We will need a clear description of the fieldsite that will make it comprehensible for readers who are new to it or may never have come across it while it was in vogue. We want our writing to have some longevity, and hopefully the theoretical and conceptual importance will make our writings about the Internet more than simply part of the historical record.

We want people in the future to be able to read our writing and get something out of it, even if the particular technology we are talking about is no longer popular.

- *What did I do?* Readers need to know how the data were generated. If qualitative interviews have been carried out using the Internet, it will be important to contextualize the results with a discussion of how the interview was carried out. An interview is more than simply an occasion for participants to tell us what they think. An interview is a carefully crafted social encounter (Rapley 2001), and any accounts produced have to be understood as shaped by the specificities of that social encounter. Readers of qualitative research reports will therefore often want to know in detail about the context within which respondent accounts were generated, including details of the setting, the means we take to keep the conversation flowing and put participants at their ease, and the extent to which we offered encouragement, feedback, and disclosure about our own thoughts and agenda. Similarly, ethnographic research can often be adaptive to emerging circumstances, and the decisions that we make as we go along shape the final "field" that we describe. Readers do not need to know about every twist and turn that the research took, but they need to have some idea of how our agency shaped the research outcomes. The lack of a standardized research instrument in qualitative research means that we have a responsibility to explore how we shaped the research encounter in particular directions.

- *How did I do my analysis?* A part of the methodological discussion that is often omitted, or skated over, is the process of analysis that the researcher used to make sense out of the mass of data. In this regard, there is often a reluctance to admit just how fortuitous and subjective the process can be. Some researchers will use a specified approach, such as grounded theory (Glaser & Strauss 1967), but this approach is cited far more often than it is actually used in its full form (Hodkinson 2008). If you used grounded theory, then this process should be discussed; but if not, then it should not be invoked. Rather than looking for a particular "brand named" approach to analysis, it can be more effective to cite precedents who used similar analytic approaches. Texts such as Silverman's (2006) overview of modes of qualitative analysis demonstrate the wealth of different, theoretically tailored approaches to analysis of various forms of qualitative data. It is helpful, therefore, to describe exactly how your findings emerged from the data and what you did to facilitate their emergence.

These observations may not be contained in a separate "methods" section of a report. Sometimes, an overly detailed discussion of methods spoils the flow of a monograph for the general reader, and the methodological discussion will be relegated to an appendix. It is important, however, that this discussion be there somewhere. First, the researcher has a responsibility to quite precisely lay out the boundaries and limitations of what he or she has done, as well as its strengths. Second, in qualitative research, we learn our techniques very often from what other researchers have done. There is no rule-book to instruct us in our adaptive and creative set of methods, and these detailed accounts of what other researchers have done are extremely helpful to fuel our own methodological imaginations.

Taking the Reader to the Research Setting

As described above, it is very important that a research report tells the reader exactly what we are basing our account upon. At the same time, however, most qualitative writers want their writing to be more creative than a blunt account of what we did and what the outcomes were, and, in particular, they want to use their creativity to help their readers experience something of the research setting. As qualitative writers, we convince our readers not by an array of statistical tests or a wealth of graphs and charts, but by writing that helps readers feel that we really understand our setting in depth and that they can share in that understanding. In this section, I explore some of the devices used in qualitative writing about the Internet to help readers develop an understanding of the setting. I will be drawing on three key examples: Lori Kendall's (2002) *Hanging Out in the Virtual Pub*, a ethnographic study of a text-based virtual reality called a MUD,[1] Shani Orgad's (2005b) interview- and observation-based study of the use of online spaces by breast cancer patients, and Bonnie Nardi's (2010) anthropology of the graphical game World of Warcraft.[2] These examples will help me to illustrate some of the different devices used in ethnographic and interview-based qualitative writing about the Internet. This is not, however, intended as an exhaustive account, but more a stimulation to the writer's imagination, and it is very much up to each author to use whatever makes sense to give readers an authentic feel for the particular setting they have in mind.

As described in the introductory chapter, ethnographers often use an "arrival story" to describe how they got into the field, and this offers readers a frame for interpreting what follows. The arrival story describes how the ethnographer first arrived in the setting and how it seemed to them, often giving both an evocation of the kind of experience that the setting offered and a glimpse of the theoretical interests that the experience triggered for them. Arrival stories also help to convince us that the ethnographer was really there and has a stock of valid experience upon which to base his or her theoretical insights. Such arrival stories often occur in accounts of Internet-based fieldwork, and they serve very similar purposes to those used in describing more conventional anthropological fieldwork settings (Pratt 1986).

Nardi (2010), for example, begins her text with a prologue that describes how she was first introduced to World of Warcraft:

I listened when students talked about video games in casual conversation. Colourful but unfamiliar names jangled in my brain: *EverQuest, Ultima Online, Final Fantasy, Guild Wars.* The

---

1. A MUD, or multiuser dungeon, was a text-based form of online social space that was used for synchronous interactions. In that, it was similar to a chat room, but differed in that the environment and the participants were also described in text. Some MUDs were purely social, while others were used for role-playing games.
2. World of Warcraft is a multiplayer online game in which players are visually represented by an avatar, interacting with other participants in real-time through game graphics, text-based chat, and audio channel. Players collaborate in guilds to achieve goals in the game.

game that kept coming up was *World of Warcraft*. Based on this highly unscientific sampling, I decided to try out *WoW*, as it is known, to further my broad research goal of studying social life on the Internet. In December of 2005, I signed up for an account with Blizzard Entertainment, the maker of the game, and began to play. I planned to play for a few months until I knew enough to conduct some interviews. I didn't expect to like the game—I had played board games as a child and found them uninteresting. I tried to prevent my own children from playing video games, which I considered a waste of time.

When I sat down with *World of Warcraft*, I had no idea of what to do. Luckily my son Christopher was home from college for Christmas break. He helped me create an animated character with which to adventure in the three-dimensional virtual world. Despite my anti-game campaign, Christopher had played text-based online role-playing games, and, although he was not familiar with *World of Warcraft*, he seemed to understand basic game semantics. We set forth on a quest. "Click on the monster and right click!" he suggested. I obeyed. My frantic clicking produced the salutary effect of killing the monster (which would soon have killed my character). Such activity seemed inordinately silly, but I was secretly smitten with the beautiful *WoW* graphics and charmed to be a character called a Night Elf. Nardi (2010, 4)

The account goes on to describe Nardi's dawning realization of the extent of social contact and cooperation between players. This account sets us up to expect a text that explores the social and aesthetic attractions of the online gaming experience. It also, I would argue, positions Nardi as a very particular kind of ethnographer who has assured us that she came to the setting as a stranger not already sympathetic to the socially interactive qualities of online games. Her subsequent descriptions of World of Warcraft as "new means of forming and sustaining human relationships and collaborations through digital technology" (Nardi 2010, 5) are thus rendered all the more convincing because we have been assured that she was not expecting them. She suspects that readers might also be skeptical about how real the social bonds formed through online gaming might be, and by describing her own revelatory experience she prepares us for one of our own.

An arrival story is therefore useful in providing a narrative start to get readers into the setting and offers them a way to think about it that might go against their preconceptions. It can show how the researcher came to his or her topic with an open mind. Implicitly, the writing resists the reader's imagined accusation that predrawn conclusions have been imposed on the researcher's fieldwork experiences. Indeed, ethnographers often make a point of describing instances in which their preconceptions were overturned or where they had to rethink an analytic framework because these surprises help to reassure us that the field has an agency to resist inappropriate theorizing.

A writer describing Internet interactions cannot assume that the reader automatically knows what his or her "experience" is actually like. It is often, therefore, useful to offer a brief account of what taking part in the particular online interaction being described actually entails. Nardi (2010), for example, has an early chapter entitled "What Is World of Warcraft and Who Plays It?" This chapter gives her the chance to offer some key demographic facts about players, to describe the skills needed to play the game, to tell us what the sensory experience of the player is, and also to explore how playing is organized in time. She gives an account of a "day in the life" from her experiences with World of Warcraft, which helps us to see the interdependencies between players and the extent to which they coordinate with one another. This chapter is light on theory, focusing on giving us an introduction to how it is to be in this particular fieldsite.

Rather than giving us an arrival story grounded in the minutiae of how the online setting is achieved, Kendall (2002) begins with an attempt to evoke the style of the interaction. She describes a visit to the pub, recounting details of the setting, the people who hang out there, and the jokey style of friendly interaction that goes on. She offers us a description that could be about a face-to-face setting, before going on to explain that actually the interactions she is describing take place in an online text-based environment rather than a real-world pub. She thus frames for us the kind of setting we will be hearing about through invoking the common cultural trope of the "pub," before she moves into describing how that setting is achieved through the technology of the MUD in online space. Implicitly, she, too, heads off a reader who might be thinking that this kind of interaction isn't properly social or should not be taken seriously. In the next chapter, "Logging On: An Introduction to Blue Sky," she offers an account of the history, demographics, and practical process of using the MUD that forms the focus of the study. Just like Nardi (2010), Kendall (2002) does not assume that we know in advance what the setting is or how it feels to use a MUD, and also carefully details what makes this particular MUD different from others as a fieldsite.

Orgad's (2005b) study differs somewhat from Nardi's (2010) and Kendall's (2002) in that there is no defined fieldsite. She still, however, has to tell us where the interactions that she studied originated. Orgad (2005b) studied the online storytelling of breast cancer patients, and while she engages in some preliminary observation of discussion forums and websites, most of her study is based on direct interactions, both via e-mail and face-to-face, with women that she recruited from these settings. She is able to assume a certain familiarity among her readers about how a website works and what e-mail feels like to use: she has, however, to describe quite carefully the "landscape" of breast cancer patients' online communication because this helps to contextualize the stories that she goes on to analyze. The study that she conducts is situated in time, both within a particular moment of the understanding of cancer as a cultural object, and within a particular understanding of the use of the Internet. In particular, the genre of personal websites telling the owner's story has now been supplanted somewhat by various forms of blogging and social networking, so it is very important for the longevity of her account and the specificity of her analysis that Orgad (2005b) tells us how it was at the particular time when her data were collected.

In addition to the contextualization of her study in a particular cultural moment, Orgad (2005b) also attends to the more mundane but still very important methodological issues, including in her book an appendix with the demographic details of participants and also an account of the process of recruiting participants and the attendant concerns about representativeness and preserving an ethical stance of anonymity. She has also reflected very effectively on the process of moving between online and offline interactions with participants, and the extent to which these different interactions are mutually contextualizing, with neither necessarily treated as the gold-standard "real" account of how participants feel (Orgad 2005a).

Each of these authors quite carefully introduces readers to their fieldsite or research focus without assuming that it will already be familiar or recognizable. They give their studies longevity by carefully describing what the Internet was like at the time their study was done and by telling readers in detail what the technology that they are describing feels like to use. By showing how they came to the fieldsite, they establish themselves as appropriately experienced to tell us about it, but still as having been sufficiently open-minded to have acquired an authentic experience to tell.

Interweaving Theory and Data

Having established the nature of the fieldsite and the credentials of the author as a fieldworker, qualitative writing about the Internet usually moves into a more theoretically dense mode, establishing in a series of thematic sections or chapters the key contributions to knowledge that the author wants to make. Even in these more theoretically oriented sections, however, data will often feature heavily in the writing. Evocative descriptions, arrival stories, and careful methodological accounts of particular Internet technologies in cultural context play a key role in taking readers to the research setting and helping them see what it might mean to be there. Beyond the various descriptive accounts based on the experiences of the researcher, the inclusion in the text of materials from the field helps to increase the readers' feelings that they know exactly what it is like.

By allowing the reader to see the raw material, or read a direct quotation from what the participant said, the writer allows the readers a more direct experience of the field and empowers them to make their own judgments about the interpretation. By empowering the reader to make his or her own assessment, the writer can actually increase the trust that readers have in the writer's interpretations (provided the interpretations are, indeed, found to be plausible). Including materials direct from the field often helps the text to be more interesting and feel more authentic (I have often been guilty of skimming through a text, reading all of the quotations from interviews and excerpts of data first, before returning to the beginning to follow the theoretical narrative). The data give a quick insight into the world being described, which readers can situate in context of other worlds they already know about and this helps to ground the theoretical narrative. Maybe other readers are more disciplined about following the path set out by the author than I, but still, the strong presence of data interwoven with theory is an important feature of qualitative writing.

Nardi (2010) describes a highly graphically rich environment and therefore includes screenshots from key pieces of interaction to illustrate her account, together with quotations from chat logs and from interviews with participants. Orgad (2005b) quotes at length from interviews, both online and face-to-face, together with material from websites carefully edited to preserve the anonymity of participants. Orgad (2005b) and Kendall (2002) both note that the various different sources from which they quote can be confusing for readers, and they make use of different fonts and styles for quotations from different sources. As in most qualitative research writing, the words of participants are generally rendered with respect for the form in which they were delivered, which includes direct rendering of quotations, including any spelling mistakes or unusual grammar.

In common with most qualitative research writing, the authors described above make extensive use of direct quotations from research participants, both in setting the scene for the fieldwork and in the theoretical narrative of the main text. This practice is very similar whether we are quoting from a transcript of an audio recording from a face-to-face interview or from an e-mail interview or chat room log. We will have data available from recordings of direct interactions in the field that show what research participants said to us. We will also often have documents to draw on in our writing: in a conventional fieldwork setting, a researcher will often collect documents such as reports, publicity leaflets, letters, advertisements, and diaries, and these documents collected in the field can be quoted in illustration of theoretical points. In Internet research, the collected documents may threaten to overwhelm the researcher, since it is so easy to access archives, download websites, or save other forms of electronic file. All of this collected material is available to be subjected to thematic analysis and quoted in illustration of descriptions of the field. The volume of material available can be a challenge (and can prompt a turn to quantitative techniques, as described in the next chapter). The principles of developing a theoretically informed narrative and using data from the accounts of participants and the documents that they generate in illustration of theoretical points are, however, relatively similar between Internet research and research in other settings.

It is important to remember when structuring a piece of qualitative writing—whether about the Internet or any other subject—that quotations from data are there to illustrate the analysis, rather than substitute for the analysis. The overall points to be made and the theoretical "plot" that structures the report need to be established first; only then are fragments of data chosen to illustrate the point. It is all too easy to string a research report around a few juicy quotations without taking care to consider how representative these particular quotations are of the body of data as a whole. A report based on a few quotations without the underpinning of a detailed thematic analysis will rarely be able to develop a significant engagement with theory or make confident assertions about patterns and structures in the data. Even if a piece of research is not based on a thorough application of grounded theory, it still needs to be more than a story about a few bits of data that struck the researcher's attention.

It follows from the above that the plot of a piece of qualitative writing needs to be planned out carefully in advance. Often, when we are carrying out fieldwork, particular incidents strike us as noteworthy and we may build a section of the report around them. Still, though, these vignettes need to serve a particular function within the overall narrative. A graduate student I was supervising taught me a valuable rule of thumb that she had been given by another student: write down in advance what three main points you want a chapter to make. As you further plan sections and subsections within the chapter, think again about the three main points you want to make at each level. Sometimes there may be four points, sometimes two, but three main points work surprisingly often as the skeleton for a chapter and its subsections. The crucial point is that planning out the key components of your argument helps you to stick to making them, rather than drifting around in a sea of interesting thoughts.

The balance between theory and data in a report will vary depending on the audience and the use that they are expected to make of what they read. Sometimes, the emphasis is more on a rich description of the responses of a particular set of people than on making a theoretical contribution to academic knowledge, particularly when a piece of qualitative research is intended to inform policy interventions. Zwaanswijk et al. (2007), for example, report on an online focus group looking at preferences in communication among childhood cancer patients and their parents. Here, the data take center stage because the research is intended to inform the development of approaches to communication that fit better with what this group of patients and their families want.

Being in a medical journal, Zwaanswijk et al.'s (2007) paper has a quite conventional structure for a research article: the methods section includes tables on the characteristics of participant and the questions asked, and it summarizes the characteristics of responses in terms of how many contributions there were and how often people participated. These details flesh out for us the circumstances under which the data were generated. The paper also summarizes an initial thematic coding across different categories of respondent. The main results section of the paper then consists of a thematic discussion using quotations to illustrate different themes arising from the data, in very similar style to many reports on face-to-face focus groups. The discussion combines generalizations about patterns of response with specific examples:

> Survivors emphasized that young patients should be explicitly involved in deciding how they should be informed and which information they should receive. This may also bring about some difficulties, as a survivor (aged 19) stated: *'I don't think asking a child to indicate what he or she wants or doesn't want to know will work out right. There may be a lot of information that you would like to know, but you may not even know that it exists. Particularly at the start. You shouldn't make a child think too much at that time, because he or she is thinking of other things then.'* (Zwaanswijk et al. 2007)

The paper offers a structured, yet richly evocative account of the patterns of response to the questions asked by the researchers. The fact that the data were generated via an online focus group was very important at the stage of conducting the research and helped to make it viable to include a wide range of participants in different circumstances. But this actually becomes less relevant in the research report, which simply focuses on what people said (or rather, typed) and the lessons to be learned.

Thus far, the practices of qualitative writing about the Internet are fairly similar to other forms of qualitative writing. However, the notion of direct quotation of data does take on a new significance with Internet research, since, in many online settings, the interaction is "self-transcribing" in that a log file or archive of messages can be saved by the researcher. In a conventional, face-to-face setting, an ethnographer wanting to describe a sequence of actions would have to put the observation of events into their own words, as fieldnotes, unless there happened to be a participant account to draw upon. By contrast, the possibility of keeping logs of online interactions, whether from a chat room, MUD, or World of Warcraft raid, seems to offer up the chance to draw on apparently impartial, direct accounts of action in qualitative Internet writing. The log file gives the writer the chance to show how events unfolded as an objective phenomenon, before offering an analytic account of what went on. Taking the reader to the setting can, therefore, apparently be achieved in a very direct way. Here, for example, is a snippet of interaction between students (using anonymized nicknames) in one of my online seminars, chosen to evoke the informal melee of interactions going on:

692: cmc[3] you can pretend to be someone completely different

chrishine: sure—although it would be hard to sustain a fake identity

but there are cases

781: which is quite scary, you can be anyone you want including describing looks and potentially personality as you can be more forward, happier, sadder, cheeky etc

497: ye so u can b who they want u to be even if ur not

692: ftf you have so many things to annalyse when u are talking to someone that becomes second nature but it also means you can read their body lang and things

497: and more time to think of your response

chrishine: some people like it precisely because it brings out a different side of their personality being online

576: get more of a chance to rthink of something good to say

---

3. CMC, computer-mediated communication.

513: or you can be your real self, let out emotions that you would normally repress due to being shy, etc.

576: haha

chrishine: so if you read walther's paper[4] you find there are 4 things he thinks make cmc different to ftf

692: its not continual conversation though, because you can do other things and not reply straight away like in a ftf convo

chrishine: 1. CMC is editable—we can change our minds and try to get it just right

692: yea

chrishine: 2. More time can be spend composing and refining a message than in a face to face situation

3. Writers are physically separated from readers, and so can filter out involuntary cues and just present the content and emotions they want to present

497: have be talking to loads of different people at the same time...

692: thats what is wrong with cmc, time to think over a sentence is unnatural

chrishine: 4. In CMC more effort is free to attend to composing the message in CMC, rather than thinking about other factors in the environment and behaving appropriately

maybe cmc is the new natural 692?

296: i think a problem with cmc is what ive got now, im reading but beofre i can reply to one thing, something else is said, so i end up not commenting back and thinking about the next thing that has been said!

497: yeah surely ftf is more your 'true self' as its what comes naturally

chrishine: i know 296, it is really tricky to keep a coherent conversation going

---

4. Walther (2007).

497: yeh you have to act fast in a group conversation, it's hard

692: i dont think it can be, how is planning when and how you are going to talk natural

781: i think its difficult to keep up with conversation as people interact with different comments and different conversations go on

497: everyone just throws ideas out there, you can't type fast enough...

chrishine: i feel bad because i don't acknowledge everything people say

which a good teacher should

sorry if anyone feels ignored:(

692: that is why this is not a natural or good way of talking to people

:)

Log files and screen shots do have a major part to play in qualitative Internet writing because they help to evoke the setting for readers and often show more than the authors who include them as illustrations can comment upon directly. Their apparent objectivity can, however, often be an illusion, since the actual experience of Internet interactions is in practice highly personal, being dependent on particular combinations of technologies and connection speeds, not to mention the attention of the user and the various other forms of distraction and multitasking that may be going on. A huge experiential difference exists between being there as an online event happens and reading a log file of it afterward or looking at a screenshot. Part of the significance of the reflexive aspect of qualitative Internet research, as I will discuss in the next section, is in filling in some of the experience of being there that logs and archives miss out. Tempting as it is, then, we cannot necessarily take the log file as the objective account of events as anyone present might have experienced them. However, when selectively used, log files do offer an interesting resource for qualitative Internet writing because they allow us to take the reader to the setting in a new way.

A log file can be a very useful resource for qualitative Internet research because it captures interaction for review later, like the audio recording of a face-to-face interview. Just like the audio recording, it is not the experience itself, but it makes something of the experience durable in time and allows it to be juxtaposed with other experiences. Log files are often not particularly useful for inclusion in research reports without extensive editing, however. Multiple conversations often interweave, and portions of conversation relevant to the analytic point that we want to make will be interspersed with material that is irrelevant and confusing for the current purpose. Kendall (2002), for example, carefully edits down most of the quotations from log files that she uses in her main text, for the purposes of intelligibility. In an appendix, she includes an unedited log file to illustrate how the interactions actually unfolded.

A final aspect of taking the reader to the research setting involves the use of analogies with more familiar settings to give the reader a hook for understanding what the online site is like. I have already described Kendall's use of the metaphor of the pub to evoke the kind of interaction that she encountered in the MUD. She goes on to make use of other metaphors, such as the locker room, to explore particular forms of masculinity enacted by those in the setting.

For readers who may be unfamiliar with online games such as World of Warcraft, Nardi discusses similarities with dance clubs, paintballing, and historical re-enactment to evoke the enjoyment of visual performance within the game, before turning to a quotation from a player who describes it as like "baseball in elf costumes" (Nardi 2010, 54) to capture the combination of competition and performance experienced by participants. Such analogies help to fix what the experience is like for nonplaying readers and can also open up interesting theoretical avenues for exploration. Analogies are particularly useful in qualitative Internet writing because they help to tell us how to feel about a setting, beyond the specific technical details of what interaction there entails.

Anonymity, Confidentiality, and Data Presentation

I have described above the interweaving of theory and data that characterizes qualitative writing and explored the ways in which data from Internet based fieldwork and interviews can be used to evoke the setting for readers and to illustrate theoretical points. Data often occupy a very prominent place in qualitative writing, and the qualitative Internet researcher often has an abundance of data to draw upon. Some forms of Internet-derived data can, however, be problematic to include in research reports because they impinge on the privacy of the subjects of the research. As discussed in the sections on research design and ethics in the previous chapter, the public availability of data on the Internet does not mean that such data are automatically available for research. People using the Internet may not necessarily be aware of the multiple possible audiences for their words and actions, and may certainly not have imagined that they were making themselves available as research subjects simply by using the Internet. It is therefore unwise of authors to assume that just because they have found data on the Internet, they can quote it in a research report.

The use of social networking sites, video uploading, and various forms of blogging and micro-blogging have been described as suffering from the problem of "context collapse" (Marwick & boyd 2011), in which people make their utterances on the Internet to indeterminate and unimaginably multiple audiences. It seems unfair to argue that people should have known their words were being uttered in public and therefore fair game for research, given that it is so hard to develop any meaningful sense of who might be out there at all. Marwick and boyd (2011) argue that Twitter users develop a diverse array of heuristics for imagining who they might be tweeting to, but few of these are based on concrete evidence or rational assessment. Such uncertainty among Internet users about the meaningful public for their words and actions means that researchers must be very careful what they treat as data. Ethically speaking, it becomes important for researchers to attend not just to the fact of availability, but also to the means by which those producing data make sense of their actions, whether these attitudes are justified, technically speaking, or not.

When materials have been generated through direct interaction with participants, such as in e-mail interviews or online focus groups, it can probably be assumed that these words are available to be quoted in research reports, provided that standard informed consent procedures at the time of the interaction were followed. Sometimes, there will be a distinction between material used to inform the analysis and material available to be quoted directly in research reports. Flicker et al. (2004), for example, created an online message board for the purposes of their research, but in their report only quoted directly from postings written by teenagers who had explicitly consented to be part of their study, using as background material to be considered in analysis, but not quoted, those postings written by teens who had not consented.

Even when consent has been given to use data for analysis and to quote it in reports, usual qualitative writing practice would remove identifying details and use pseudonyms for research participants. For Internet research, this convention often means changing not only real names (if these were ever known) but also screen names, usernames, and avatar names, since people often have a considerable investment in their online reputation. Some researchers also change the identifying details of the setting of their research, such as the chat room, guild, or MUD. In Nardi's (2010) book, for example, the references to guilds within which she played, the members of those guilds, and the characters that they played are pseudonyms. She does, however, quote from interactions between players and material posted to game-related websites, on the basis that these are publicly available texts, and she does give links to the full versions of some of the player postings that she excerpts.

Kendall (2002) also gives pseudonyms to the MUD that she studied and the participants within the MUD. She took account of the potential responses to her writing by distributing draft copies of the dissertation among participants, and took on board their corrections to her version of the group history and some interpretations of events. Clearly, although she might be hiding the identity of the group to protect against idle curiosity from outsiders, members of the group would readily be able to identify one another. Indeed, she found that some members delighted in decoding the pseudonyms in the dissertation and even publicly posted a key to the names, thus threatening her attempts to grant them anonymity. It is, therefore, not always the case that the researcher is fully in charge of whether identities are disclosed, and they may have to be wary of the prospect that their research will be taken out of context and used for unintended purposes, possibly by participants themselves. Possibly for this reason, Miller takes a very careful approach to constructing the case studies on which he bases his observations about Facebook:

The first part of this book consists of twelve portraits. These are all based on research but, with one exception, I have made extensive changes in detail and combined materials from different participants within individual portraits in order to protect the anonymity of those who participated in the study. (Miller 2011, xi)

As a part of preserving the anonymity of his participants, Miller also explains that he took care to defriend[5] them on Facebook itself before publication.

Anthropologists have long had to face up to the fact that their works may be read not just by an academic audience, but by the very people that they have written about (Brettell 1996). When the research subjects are on the Internet, the boundaries of different genres of writing may become blurred, and it may be all the more likely that the people who we are writing about will be able to access what we say. We may be intervening much more directly in their worlds through our writing than we might have realized. We need, therefore, to pay careful attention to the extent to which the analysis that we offer, taken in conjunction with potentially searchable fragments of data, might enable people to find what we have said and apply it to themselves or to known others. Often, our response may be that the analysis is a generalization not aimed at any individual, but it cannot be assumed that it will be taken in this way. Some authors very carefully adapt even quoted material so that it cannot readily be searched back to its source. Wilkinson and Thelwall (2010) argue that even when a researcher may feel that data collected from the Internet are publicly available and usable for research purposes, the final report should still take care to protect the privacy of subjects by obscuring their identity.

The persistence of archives of Internet material across time means that it can be difficult to assess just how sensitive material from a long time ago might be now to the people who produced it. I encountered this situation when researching the history of Internet use among a group of biologists (Hine 2008b). I found that I wanted to use in my analysis some messages sent to the

---

5. "Defriending" involves removing the visible link between one's Facebook profile and the former "friend"—often this would signify the ending of a positive relationship, but in this case it was aimed at removing any trace of who the specific participants were who informed Miller's descriptions.

professional mailing list maintained by this group of biologists many years ago. The archives were still searchable and, in a sense, publicly available, but I was conscious that by citing these old messages I would be drawing a new kind of attention to them. By selectively bringing these particular messages forward in time, I would be risking embarrassment for those who had written them, and I could even be damaging their professional reputations. I also found that the group was becoming interested in my writings about them, and so there was a strong chance that whatever I wrote would be read by someone who recognized the person whom I was writing about.

To deal with the potential upset that could be caused to the people whom I was writing about, I opted for a cautious approach to quoting data. Rather than opting for a system of disguised data and pseudonyms, instead I opted to ask permission from the author for each of the messages that I wished to quote. This was time-consuming, and it was often quite a surprise for the author to be contacted about a message written many years ago, but the responses were mainly positive and often led to further research contacts, discussions about the topic of the message, and updates on what the author had done since. What began as a necessary ethical chore turned into a fruitful and enjoyable part of the research.

The decisions that authors take about the use of data and the extent to which participants are contacted and are identifiable vary considerably according to the setting and circumstances of the research. Visual materials can be particularly challenging to include in research reports. On the one hand, facial characteristics are (not yet) as readily searchable as names, but, on the other hand, we cannot obscure the identity of a face and still leave it visible as a face as easily as we can change a name. Maybe it is for this reason that there is still very little visual material in many research reports, even though it is now much easier to include figures in publications than it once was, and so many settings that are written about do have such rich visual qualities. Chou et al. (2011) are unusual in giving the full links to the YouTube videos of cancer survivors whom they analyze on the basis that they are publicly available. When visual material is not publicly available in the first place, and when its use raises some privacy issues, it is simply much harder to believe that such material can be appropriately anonymized, and it can feel more respectful to participants to leave it out. It can also be problematic to ensure that appropriate copyright permissions are in place to use visual data in a publication. The copyright issue can be particularly significant when data have been generated through use of commercial software, such as a gaming site.

boyd (2007) uses illustrative materials drawn from the MySpace profiles of participants in her ethnographic studies of social networking sites. In her thesis, she describes the reservations she has about quoting from material that may be publicly available, technically speaking, but which the teenagers who created it may not have ever considered interesting to anyone outside of their personal network. She describes her decision to remove identifying traces, to alter materials she used to make them impossible to locate using search engines, and to use such material rarely and cautiously (boyd 2008, 86). Strano (2008) includes a sample Facebook profile in her paper on the choice of profile photographs, but is careful to obscure identifying details and blank out the eyes of the head-and-shoulders photograph to render it less identifiable (although one assumes that the subject would still recognize him- or herself). Dalsgaard (2008) begins his article on self-presentation in Facebook by showing his own profile on the site, with the identifying details of friends and contributors to his news feed obscured. He then goes on to illustrate his argument about the nature of the self by referring to Facebook material relating to already-public figures such as Barack Obama, this time without obscuring identifying details.

In sensitive areas, and particularly when the researchers feel that the research agenda may not be received well by participants, some researchers have adopted a covert or semi-covert stance. For example, Cantó-Milà and Seebach (2011) carried out a study of pro-ana websites,[6] in which they justify a semi-covert stance both through their use of a discourse analytic approach (often thought to be less intrusive than analysis that focuses its commentary on the individual) and through the potential benefits of a greater understanding of these sites for the treatment of anorexia. They therefore position their research as of low risk to participants and of considerable potential benefit. In their report, they carefully alter identifying details and make use only of materials from

---

6. Websites that promote or support anorexia

publicly accessible areas of web forums. The research was not confined to these publicly accessible areas: the researchers did have access to password-protected areas of website that were shown to them by two gatekeepers who were legitimate members of the sites. The researchers declined the opportunity to use the passwords of their gatekeepers for continued access and did not use any of this material in their report. They thus trod a very careful ethical line, in which they pursued their overall research goal but attempted to avoid both deceit and harm to the users of the websites.

Markham (2006) discusses the links among methods, ethics, and reflexivity. She considers that particularly perplexing issues in negotiating an ethical research practice may arise in Internet research, in which it may be unclear exactly how existing codes of ethical research practice apply. She argues for a reflexive attitude to research ethics, in which we focus on making contextually appropriate decisions and on trying to see and respond to the politics embedded in research situations. This is a useful approach to take in writing qualitative Internet research, in which the researcher has to build on his or her emerging knowledge of the research setting itself in order to decide on what approach to take to informed consent and to the inclusion of identifiable research materials in reports. This emergent, reflexive research ethics may be challenging to maintain in the face of requirements from ethical review committees that we make statements about our research practices in advance, but it is an inevitable consequence of the adaptive nature of qualitative methods, the emergent nature of Internet practice, and the post-data-collection analytic focus of qualitative theorizing.

Reflexivity

Qualitative research cannot help but be partial, in two senses. First, whatever our aspiration to be comprehensive, we can never study the whole of a situation or understand an entire cultural domain. Life is not neatly bounded in such a way as to allow us to study the "whole" of anything, and our resources are always limited. Qualitative studies will therefore encounter dilemmas, experience constraints, and set boundaries (Roberts & Sanders 2005; Hine 2008a), and the resulting reports will have an inherently limited perspective. Second, our research reflects our own allegiances and experiences, and so is, in this sense, if not overtly partisan, at least not wholly impartial. Taking both of these senses of partiality together, it is clear that our research will be to some extent contingent and that the qualitative writing that we do will reflect a particular worldview and set of choices. For these reasons, a reflexivity that considers who we are and how we come to know what we do forms an important part of contemporary qualitative writing. In response to the "crisis of representation" (Denzin 1997) in ethnography, reflexive musings on the contingency of the research object became a significant move in undermining the apparent objectivity of the text and putting the researcher's agency into the spotlight. Fabian positions this, rather than being a postmodern turn, as part of a recognition that ethnography was a very particular kind of knowledge: "To make our writing look subject- and author-less was to misrepresent what happens during ethnographic research and writing" (Fabian 1991, xi). These positions on reflexivity in qualitative research writing in general form a backdrop for thinking about specific aspects of reflexivity that come to the fore in qualitative writing about the Internet.

As described in the previous chapter, many research designs involving the Internet will be preliminary and subject to change during the course of the research because we cannot know in advance what will be the relevant aspects to follow up in order to make sense of the situation. Our final research object will be shaped by choices made, paths not followed, practical constraints, and theoretical predilections. A prominent aspect of many qualitative research reports is, therefore, a sense of the contingency of the report. Although standing confidently and reporting on what they did, felt, and saw, at the same time qualitative Internet researchers can usefully include in their reports reflections on how these things could have been otherwise. This includes, as Markham (2006) suggests, thinking about the balance between convenience and representativeness for a particular purpose that shapes a choice of fieldsite or interview population. Similarly, it is useful to reflect on qualities of the researcher and his or her prior experiences that influence the relationships formed, the questions asked, and the themes emerging from data. As Roberts and Sanders (2005) suggest, many dilemmas and constraining factors will be experienced before, during, and after the research, and these will have a major influence on the research object that emerges.

These forms of reflexivity, highlighting the contingency of the research object, are continuous with other forms of qualitative research writing. However, there are also some very specific forms of reflexivity that turn it into a research tool for qualitative Internet research in particular. When research focuses on mediated relationships, the researcher may often be limited in his or her understanding of other participants. If the medium that the researchers seeks to understand is also the medium through which the research is conducted, it can be difficult to gain a full comprehension, from the accounts of participants, of what it is that they are experiencing. Under these circumstances, reflexivity is an invaluable asset. If it is difficult for qualitative Internet researchers to know how respondents are feeling, and if it seems difficult to make relationships or resolve uncertainties, the researcher can usefully reflect on whether his or her respondents are also experiencing these concerns. Rather than immediately leaping to try to resolve the uncertainty by meeting respondents face-to-face, it is worth taking time to reflect on whether living with uncertainty is an inherent part of the experience in this particular use of the Internet. Qualitative Internet researchers can, therefore, use reflection on the experience of forming mediated relationships to fill in some of the inevitable gaps in their understanding that come from not being able to exist beyond the screen with all of the people who feature in the research, in their other contexts.

Reflexivity, then, is very important in qualitative Internet research because it involves us in reflecting on how mediated interactions feel and in understanding what it takes to participate in them effectively. When uncertainty seems to be placing difficulties in the path of drawing concrete conclusions, it is worth reflecting on whether the existence of that uncertainty is a conclusion in its own right. Reflexivity can play a significant part in online ethnographies as the ethnographer focuses on the embodied experience of being online and reflects on the various circumstances that shape and constrain online experiences. Markham (1998) uses a strongly autoethnographic approach to explore the experience of using the Internet, identifying the coexistence of perceptions of the Internet as a tool, a place, and a mode of being. It becomes clear that we cannot assume that we know how other people experience the Internet, thus leaving an indeterminacy in Internet-mediated qualitative research that cannot ultimately be filled (just as we cannot ever know fully what a face-to-face encounter means to the other party), but that can be addressed to some extent by careful reflection on our own responses. As Rybas and Gajjala (2007) describe it, this "epistemology of doing" becomes highly significant when the research focuses on the construction of digital identities. Pearce (2009) displays this particularly effectively in a reflection on the social construction of the ethnographer and the limits to self-determination of identity in online settings.

How far an account should dwell on reflexivity or digress into autoethnography can be controversial. Autoethnographies can be critiqued for celebrating the ethnographer's perspective to excess, and it is all too risky within Internet research for the lack of instant visual feedback to encourage ignoring the different experiences of other users and treating the ethnographers' experience as if everybody is the same. I am, however, by no means arguing that all online researchers should simply use their own experience to fill in for a lack of knowledge about the experience of other participants. Notably, Nardi (2010), Kendall (2002), and Orgad (2005b) did meet with participants for offline discussions, even when their primary interest was in how online worlds were constituted. In each case, however, reflecting on the experience of being an online researcher, and on what one knows of the research setting from the online interactions alone, formed a valuable part of the research account and helped to fill out that experiential dimension that is so important in qualitative research.

Reflexivity is also important in thinking about the conditions that need to be met in order for the researcher to be an effective participant in the first place. Qualitative researchers, and ethnographers in particular, have always needed to go to considerable efforts to access their fields of research, whether through negotiating access and forming trusting relationships with participants, or through traveling to distant places, learning new languages, and becoming adept at practical skills that allow them to participate. Again, these are not simply practical difficulties that get in the way of getting on with the research, but can be important methodological moments in which the researcher learns about cultural distance and reflects on what unites and separates different cultural contexts. Internet researchers encounter somewhat different barriers, but again, their experiences of getting into the field can be an important methodological tool that deserves discussion in the final report. Being an ethnographer in an online setting often requires reaching a level of technical skill that enables participation in the required range of activities. Nardi (2010), for example, needed to be skilled enough at World of Warcraft to take part in raids with other guild members: had she not acquired that level of skill, she would have been very limited in the activities she could participate in and would have been a hindrance to the enjoyment of other players. She draws on Pearce's (2009) notion of "participant engagement" to describe the very active form that observation takes in these settings, in which the object of the research is the medium itself.

In summary, it is important in qualitative Internet writing to think carefully about your own experiences and to consider what role they can play in the analysis and in the text. Without being overindulgent, it can be very useful to reflect on how it felt to carry out your research using computer-mediated communication. This might help you to reflect more generally on the nature of the medium and also to make your writing about the medium more evocative. The reflexive element of analysis is particularly relevant to ethnographic research, but also applies to other forms of qualitative research on the Internet. When the research uses documents found on the Internet, it is useful to think about whether the way that documents were located and interpreted bears any relation to the way that an ordinary user might have found and read them. When interviews were conducted via the Internet, it is useful to think about how the encounter felt for the researcher and whether similar emotions might have been experienced by interviewees. The interview forms a very specific context in which meanings are produced, so it is important for the researcher to reflect on factors that shape that context, including the particular qualities of the medium used for the interaction.

Time and Internet Data

One very significant aspect of a reflexive insight into what experience of the Internet is like is the researcher's experience of time while in the field. Lysloff (2003) describes the solitary yet social experience of participating in an online music forum partly by reference to the temporal pacing that forms an intrinsic part of the experience: he describes night-long sessions of intense synchronous chat and e-mail, together with "disorienting moments of temporal suspension when I downloaded large files of music; these were long moments of isolation and boredom" (Lysloff 2003, 236). This kind of reference to the temporal aspects of the experience of being an Internet user is very important in locating the Internet experience in a particular context. People do not experience the Internet as free-floating digital beings: they are somewhere and somewhen, embodied people making meaning out of what they do in diverse ways. Reflecting on the experience of Internet usage as fast or slow, convenient or frustrating, part of the routine or an exceptional event, is an important part of remembering these contextualizing, meaning-giving aspects. When we look at an interview transcript, we often look at the content and forget how that content actually emerged over time; however, the pace of an interview, and the timing of any significant pauses or delays, can be quite important in shaping the experience and can tell us something quite significant about what is going on.

Classically, ethnographic texts were written as if events happened in the present, apparently presenting the knowledge of other people contained in them as if these people were always so and would continue to be so, rather than that they just happened to be so when the ethnographer was with them. This use of the present tense can give the work a timeless quality that may not be justified when we actually do not have access to the past or the subsequent events for this group. Temporality in ethnographic accounts has been much discussed (notably by Fabian 1983, Hastrup 1990, and Fabian 1991) as a choice that should be more consciously made. This is particularly so in Internet research, in which the persistence of data in various forms of archive means that the temporality of data generation can be very different to the temporality of the researcher's experience of it. It can be very easy to slip into describing Internet events as if they are happening now, even when the archives being used were generated some time ago. This temporal flattening of Internet archives presents a temptation to ignore the temporality of data generation, but, if we do so, we miss out on what can often be a very important aspect of the research.

If we are using an archive that goes a long way back in time (in Internet terms, at least), it can be important to reflect on what the Internet was like for these users at the time when the data were produced. What was it like, culturally and technically speaking, to be an Internet user then, and what were the demographics of Internet users in general, and of this setting in particular? How ordinary or exceptional might this person have held him- or herself to be? What was it sensible, ordinary, and necessary to do with the Internet at that time? What were websites and discussion forums like at the time, and what new possibilities were emerging? Reflecting on this kind of issue helps us to put ourselves into the place of the people whose words we are examining and to see them as a part of the reality that they inhabited then. Internet archive material needs to be understood as a historian understands an artifact from the past, interpreting it not through the values of the present but through the values that informed its production and reception at the time it was created.

It can be quite difficult to recover exactly what the Internet was like in all of these different ways if one did not live through it. Fortunately, there are surveys that show how the Internet population and its activities have changed over time (for example, the Oxford Internet Surveys, http://microsites.oii.ox.ac.uk/oxis/), and the WayBack machine (http://web.archive.org/) gives a stimulating insight to the way that websites have changed over time. The mass media of the day can give a fascinating insight into the construction of the Internet as a cultural artifact located in time, as I found when investigating online responses to the Louise Woodward case (Hine 2000). Beyond this, it is important simply to begin with the assumption that a particular event captured in an Internet archive made sense to those concerned at the time, and to try to excavate from the data itself exactly how it made sense, rather than imposing upon it values from the present. It would also be easy to look back in pity on the former Internet users who lacked the speed of current Internet connections, the copious graphical material, and the ease of social networking online that we take for granted now. These values, based in the present-day Internet, should not be imposed upon the practices of the past, and the activities of past Internet users should be taken on their own terms, rather than being treated as a faulty, primitive version of the contemporary Internet.

An archive of Internet discussions can, in fact, be a very useful way of exploring changing values and practices. I mentioned earlier the ethical question that arose when using archives of the professional mailing list of a group of biologists. I was using the list to give me access into the changing practices of this group over time, being particularly interested in how the Internet had been incorporated into and had potentially transformed ways of doing work (Hine 2008b). One feature of these practices that was of interest to me was the emergence of digital images to be used in making identifications by this group that had previously held that one had to examine the actual organism in order to make a reliable identification. By going back through the message archives, I was able to find very early instances of a digital image being offered up in a request for help in identification. Digital cameras were not widely available then, so an early case involved an actual (dead) fish being placed on a flatbed scanner to produce the image that was offered up for identification. This produced much hilarity among the discussion list members, but also some serious attempts at identification. By looking at the initial message and the responses around it, I was able to get a sense of this activity in its proper historical context, and I was able to track forward in time to see how the offering up of images for identification purposes and the reactions to this activity changed over time.

This use of the discussion list as if it simply reflected the concerns of the discipline at the time is, of course, not entirely justified. Any present-day discussion forum or mailing list only gives a very selective view of what a group of people think and do, and the archived discussion list is just the same. I found when I interviewed present-day list users that the readers of the list would actively interpret it, filtering what they read through their own knowledge of the discipline and using their broader social skills in working out what was going on behind the scenes in various exchanges. They knew that the people contributing to the list were only a small proportion of those working in the discipline, and often quite distinctively outspoken members at that. It is important, then, not to treat an archive as if it were some shining pearl of preserved reality. The circumstances of production may largely be lost to us and irretrievable, but this does not mean that we can simply ignore that they ever existed. It can be important for our analysis to try to recover what we can from the archive itself and from other kinds of data we can find about the time when the data were created.

Even when a fairly short time span is covered in a piece of Internet research, it can still sometimes be very useful to situate the events chronologically and to monitor their correspondence with other events. Wen and colleagues (2011) link discussion group events with the progression of disease in a woman with breast cancer and are able to show how the significance of the group for the woman concerned varies according to her experiences of the different stages of the disease. Clearly, different temporal structures will be of interest depending on the theoretical concerns of researchers. As Beaulieu and Høybye point out:

> Though the content of mailing lists is continuously shaped by the social life of the list, it is at the same time positioned in time and retained as archived material, searchable, and accessible even years past its production. For some projects, the archival time will be more appropriate while for others, the way time and timing are experienced and shaped in relation to the mailing list will be more important. It is nevertheless important to realise the diversity of temporalities at play around these technologies. (Beaulieu & Høybye, 2011, 260)

For Wen and colleagues, it was particularly of concern to note the individual temporality that shaped experience of the group. In other circumstances, researchers might be interested in the emerging culture of the group itself over time, and this aspect of temporality will dominate. Kendall (2002) studied a MUD group whose activities were situated in a particular moment of the computer industry and also in a particular post-college, early employment life stage for many of the users, as well as in a particular phase of Internet history. Her book includes a "where are they now" appendix, acknowledging the temporary and historically specific nature of the reality that she documents.

In addition to discussion list archives, temporal aspects of analysis are probably most likely to arise when blogs are used as data. The blog can be thought of as a kind of diary, often involving quite personal reflections contributed over a period of time, interspersed with comments from readers. As such, it offers considerable benefits for qualitative researchers (Hookway 2008; Snee 2010), particularly for analyzing changes over time (Herring, Scheidt, Kouper, & Wright 2006). Just as with the discussion list archive, we cannot take the blog as reflecting exactly what the person was thinking at the time, since their words are composed in consciousness of their public nature, and the very act of selecting a particular event or thought to blog about from the stream of daily thoughts and actions reflects an unknowable selection process. Nonetheless, blogs can be full of interesting material for qualitative researchers precisely because they consist of a series of insights produced at different times, rather than the cleaned-up and even more selective retrospective account we might get from an interview (Hookway 2008). Blogs make some forms of longitudinal study more feasible in qualitative research than they have been before, due to the difficulty of arranging repeated face-to-face interviews. Whether the research sets out to be longitudinal or not, the very nature of blogs as emergent accounts suggests that it will be important for the researcher to have some awareness of their temporal dimension when analyzing them.

Some aspects of temporality can be straightforwardly read from the markers contained in the message format: an e-mail message or mailing list contribution has the date on which it was sent in the header information; a blog post will be marked with the date, as will any accompanying comments; a website will often be marked with a date of production or revision. Threaded discussion groups display not simply the temporality of the individual messages, but also offer up a sense of emerging and interweaving simultaneity, as the various conversations proceed with their own rhythm. Not all kinds of temporality leave such obvious traces, however. We can see when the e-mail was sent, but we cannot see how long the sender labored over his or her words. Did he dash off a quick message in a hurry, or did he craft it carefully, choosing his words with agonized consciousness of the effects of a wrong choice? Do people read with careful attention, or do they flit from page to page, with fleeting impressions? In paying attention to the overt temporality of Internet interactions, it is, therefore, important not to lose sight of aspects of the Internet experience in time that do not leave visible traces, and, here again, the researcher's reflections on how she structures the temporality of her own Internet experience can be a useful resource.

Summary

Writing about the Internet as a fieldsite, or a place where interviews were carried out, is not necessarily hugely different from other forms of qualitative writing. Just like other qualitative writers, Internet researchers tell tales of how they arrived in the field, make analogies with other cultural settings, and use their own experiences intermingled with the accounts of informants to give a rich and evocative picture of the setting. Some interesting quirks and changes of emphasis are added by the particular qualities of digital research data, notably its persistence, replicability, scalability, and searchability (boyd 2007). This adds some possibilities in the availability of raw data to illustrate observations but raises some concerns in terms of doing justice to the expectations of privacy of the subjects of these data. In addition, the very specific technical qualities of many Internet applications, along with their relatively short-lived nature, mean that researchers may have to quite painstakingly explain just what the particular kind of Internet interaction they are focusing on provides for its users. Qualitative Internet researchers such as Markham (1998) have also made highly effective use of autoethnographic reflections to situate their studies and help their readers to understand not just what happened, but also how it felt, and how the generality of "the Internet" becomes a very specific experience for an individual in a particular time and place.

Qualitative writing is creative writing, which means that the formats for presenting it can vary dramatically. There are, however, certain things that the reader needs to know and that the researcher will often have a duty to establish. Key components of qualitative Internet writing are:

- A description of the setting that renders it real and recognizable for readers, through use of analogy, illustrative data excerpts, and rich description
- An accurate, but not necessarily exhaustive or chronological account of the research process and the contingent choices made along the way, including a clear description of the analytic process
- A precise portrayal of relevant characteristics of the research participants, to allow contextualization of the research setting and an awareness of its specificities
- A structured and appropriate interweaving of theoretical points with illustrative material. Just as in a museum, which has vast collections in reserve but only a small amount on display, the illustrative material has to be

chosen carefully to represent the treasures in reserve. It has also to be provided with a careful eye to the privacy implications for anyone generating or mentioned in such material.

- A careful description of the relevant Internet technology for nonusers, allowing the research account an audience beyond those already familiar with the specific application and extending its relevance into a future when this particular Internet technology may no longer be in general use.
- A thoughtful, but not overindulgent approach to reflexivity, using the author's reflections to enhance the evocative qualities of the text and to speculate on its specificity.
- Attention to relevant temporal dimensions of the research, making clear when events happened and what consequences their sequencing (as experienced by participants and by the researcher) has on the analysis

In this chapter, I have described the use of Internet-derived data to produce a rather conventional form of research report focused on giving the results of fieldwork, archival materials, or interviews. The Internet allows, however, for some rather different formats of research report and research interaction to be developed and allows us to play with the linear narrative, to develop more interactive forms of research report, and to cross the boundaries between qualitative and quantitative modes of analysis. It is to these more experimental forms of qualitative Internet writing that I turn in the next chapter.

4

INNOVATIVE ANALYSIS AND REPORTING IN QUALITATIVE INTERNET RESEARCH

IN THE early parts of this book, the kind of research reporting that I have been discussing has been fairly conventional. Chapter 3 talked about ways of fitting digitally derived data into the traditional formats of qualitative research reports, according to established methodological principles. Although I acknowledged that digital data offer up some new possibilities and pose some new challenges, still I focused on how to produce very familiar styles of qualitative research report based on these Internet-derived resources. However, this conventional approach does not exhaust the possibilities of digital data for qualitative research and, without throwing out the established principles altogether, considerable possibilities exist for a deeper transformation of both the process of analysis and the form of the research report. This chapter looks at some aspects of the research process that can potentially be more radically transformed in the face of digital data and online media. The chapter is based on recent examples of research using these approaches, but also builds on more broadly based suggestions that the Internet could occasion some quite significant changes to the practices of scholarship.

Contributions to the debate on consequences of digital information and new media for scholarship range from Borgman's (2007) information science–based review of the challenges to existing forms of information infrastructures posed by the migration of scholarship to the Internet to Hall's (2008) passionate plea for researchers to embrace open access in the interests of a revitalized and politically repositioned university. Each takes on board the possibilities of digital media to strike at the heart of what it is that academic researchers do and how they communicate with one another. Using online media, it becomes possible for researchers to move away from the longstanding reliance on traditional publishing houses who have provided quality assurance and have distributed academic work through paid subscriptions. It also becomes possible for the boundary between raw data and research output to become blurred, as digital formats free us from the constraints of print, and greater amounts of data in a wider array of media can be made available to readers. The convention of a linear narrative format for research reports, in which the author makes an authoritative statement to readers, is also potentially up for grabs, as hypermedia offers readers multiple paths through a text, blogging exposes the minutiae of the research process to diverse audiences, and micro-blogging compresses complex arguments into 140 characters or less.

These radically new forms of analysis and research report can seem to challenge the heart of what we take to be scholarship. By moving away from the traditional authoritative authorial statement about the way some aspect of the world is, they offer up different forms of relationship both with data (and the people whose activities come to be treated as data) and with the audiences for the research. Both research participants and readers are potentially offered a more active role, more equal in interpretive capacity with the author than previously was the case. However, there are also considerable forces encouraging conservatism in any research deployment of online media, not least the contemporary focus on research assessments based on productivity in recognized high-quality outlets. When researchers are concerned that their work needs to be rated by external bodies for its quality, when they want to be credited for making a distinctive contribution, and when the culture of their disciplines values particular forms of output, there may be a considerable reluctance to innovate. Add to this the inertia that stems from the traditional publishing infrastructure and the lack of evidence that many audiences actually want the ability to interact with raw data and create their own research narratives, and you have a long way to go before the majority of scholarship moves to radically transformed practices.

Despite this in-built inertia, a considerable amount of experimentation has occurred with use of online media in the research process, particularly in the field of Internet research itself. Researchers in new media and online culture tend to be more aware of the potential of the medium and more familiar with the possibilities than are researchers in some other fields, and are thus well positioned to experiment. Making innovative use of new media in your research can be a means of achieving distinction in this field. This kind of experimentation can also be the result of a principled stance, in which new media are deployed in an attempt to transform power relations between researcher and researched, thus responding to a situation in which those who are being researched are increasingly in a position to read what is said about them and to answer back. When I began compiling the examples of innovative practice for this chapter, I found that there were many instances in which new knowledge forms were being developed and where researchers were creatively adapting the medium to explore new ways of disseminating their work. Few as yet have become widely used, and none has reached the established, taken-for-granted nature of the journal article (or, indeed, the genomic database). Nonetheless, there are interesting glimmers of innovation, and many of them come from within Internet research.

The later sections of this chapter focus on the dissemination of research and on some forms of dissemination that creatively use new media. First, however, I focus on the analysis of data and its presentation and interpretation, for here, too, there are some interesting prospects for innovative research methods, some of which cross the qualitative–quantitative divide. The question of interpretation dogs Internet research, since often encounters will be fleeting and there may be considerable uncertainties about the identity of participants and the nature of contextual framing as it operates for the various participants in an interaction. The sheer amount of data that can be collected has prompted some researchers to combine qualitative and quantitative techniques, and to adopt various forms of visualization to explore structures in their data. The initial section of the chapter, therefore, explores the potential of mixed methods in the interpretation of Internet-derived data. Subsequent sections then focus on new media and the research report, looking first at hypermedia in qualitative research, then moving on to blogging as a research tool, and ending with the potential of micro-blogging as a means of relating to research audiences. The chapter concludes with a summary of tips to bear in mind when developing innovative approaches in qualitative Internet research and reflects on what it is that prompts us to innovate and what constrains us to stay the same in our research practice.

Interpreting and Visualizing Digitally Derived Data

Qualitative researchers have often relied to a large extent on the idea that they want to understand what people do "in context." We want to know how people's actions and words make sense within their everyday lives and as part of the social environments that they inhabit and construct (Bryman 1984). This reliance on a notion of "context" within which activities will make sense is, of course, often problematic to operationalize, theoretically speaking. It is latterly also often very difficult to operationalize "context" practically speaking, particularly for an Internet researcher who may have difficulty in working out just what the relevant contexts might be for people taking part in Internet interactions. It has been observed that an online ethnographer may not be able to access everything significant that is needed to understand participants' activities (see, for example, Paccagnella 1997). This is not, however, simply a practical issue of whether we can trust what people say about their offline lives when they are online. It also references a more fundamental issue concerning our assumptions as qualitative researchers about what the relevant contexts might be for understanding people's actions. This becomes particularly problematic given that networked fieldsites are inevitably incomplete and lacking in shared understandings of context between ethnographer and participants (Wittel 2000). It becomes very difficult to inhabit and share the frames of meaning-making that people are applying to make sense of their activities.

A recent example from my own research (Hine 2011) may illustrate this problem of inaccessibility or unknowability of relevant frames of meaning-making. I set out to study the traces that could be found on the Internet of the way that people responded to a particular television program, the *Antiques Roadshow*. This very popular program is exported from the United Kingdom to many countries around the world, some of which also produce their own domestic versions. It is, therefore, widely available to people as a familiar cultural form. The recurring format of the show consists of a series of sequences in which members of the public show their potentially valuable antiques to an expert, who gives an account of what the object is and then offers a valuation. By searching across the Internet, I found some discussion groups in which fans of the show congregated, some of them discussing their interest in antiques and some more focused on their enjoyment of the entertainment value of the show and of the experts as celebrities. I also, however, found a wide array of more isolated references to the show, not clustered around a specific interest group focused on the show but arising in the course of other activities. One such practice was a genre of humor using references to the predictable format of the show. For example, I found teenagers uploading YouTube videos in which they enacted an *Antiques Roadshow* valuation gone wrong. I also found videos of people's dogs howling along to the theme tune.

I came across these clips because of my interest in how people respond to the show. As such, I was positioned to understand these activities as part of a process of making meaning out of television viewing, and thus to interpret the YouTube videos as an example of a creative appropriation of a television format into everyday life. This was, to some extent, a reasonable way of making sense of what was going on. However, the relevant frames of meaning-making for those concerned far exceed the simple idea that they were responding to the show. To adequately understand the reasons why teenagers spend their time making and uploading humorous sketches using cultural references from their everyday lives, and the reasons why people video their dogs howling at television theme tunes, we would need to extend our research interest into the conventions of YouTube as an overarching social environment and of these specific genres within it, and also to the domestic contexts and wider social networks that these videos and the people who make them inhabit and represent. The relevant frame of meaning-making for understanding a particular YouTube video cannot be read off from the video itself, nor is it adequately subsumed by the particular analytic focus that a researcher happens to bring to it. It is, therefore, important to remember that we need to be imaginative in working out what the relevant frames of meaning-making might be and creative in finding ways to pursue those that are relevant to our research agenda.

Using the Internet to locate qualitative data, and using Internet search tools to aggregate activities that might be arising in otherwise widely separated cultural contexts, offer the qualitative Internet researcher a significant problem of interpretation. Often, this problem of interpretation can be swept aside under the claim that a researcher is studying an "online community" or other bounded social setting in online space, thus bracketing off a concern with whatever sense online activities might have in offline settings. This still, however, risks ignoring the very significant diverse meaning-making strategies that may prevail for any of the participants in the space and which may shape both what they do online and how they draw on their online experiences in their offline lives. Often, we have to simply accept and acknowledge these analytic constraints. The Internet leaves the perfect, fully holistic, idealized understanding of human practice as far off as it ever was. We have to live with studies that are bounded in some way by our own practice and acknowledge what those limits might be. The challenge that qualitative Internet researchers must face is how to present sufficient materials, interpreted in sufficient depth, to explore the particular analytic angle that the researcher focuses upon, without suggesting that this exhausts the potential interpretation of any specific fragment of data.

If Internet-derived data are often fragmentary, in the sense that such data stem not from an extended contact with a research participant in a shared context, but are rather something more fleeting or more detached from other frames of meaning-making, data are also often overwhelming in that too many such fragments are available simultaneously for the researcher to attend to them all with the level of detail and insight that qualitative research demands. It becomes very difficult for the researcher to develop the discipline to dwell in one place, analytically speaking, and to exhaust what is to be known there. In this regard, various methods for aggregating and navigating data have become particularly helpful to qualitative Internet researchers to help them to make sense of their data, to see how the data fit into a bigger picture, and to decide where to focus. The attractiveness of these methods for data aggregation and visualization to qualitative Internet research has often had the consequence of narrowing the gap or blurring the boundary between qualitative and quantitative approaches. Computer-aided qualitative data analysis software (CAQDAS) now offers many possibilities for exploring grounded approaches to coding across different sources of data, generated through use of different media (Lewins & Silver 2007). Although few CAQDAS packages allow direct import of hyperlinked web pages as yet, it is possible, via downloading web pages as text files or converting them to images, to import most forms of Internet-derived data into these software packages. This then encourages development of a systematic thematic analysis and makes it possible for qualitative researchers to work effectively with large volumes of data. Some creative possibilities have also emerged for using multimedia alongside text-based data and for synchronizing transcripts with original data sources. Latterly, some innovative approaches combining geographic information systems (GIS) and use of Google Maps and Google Earth allow for face-to-face data to be geo-located and visualized in virtual geographic space (Fielding & Cisneros-Puebla 2009), intriguingly blending face-to-face data with online resources.

Such juxtapositions of different forms of data, combining digital and geographically located sources to reveal new analytic dimensions, are an intriguing prospect in online qualitative research, which helps to offset some of the analytic challenges it poses. The researcher may juxtapose different data sources at different stages of a project or use a combination of datasets as a way of seeing a project from different angles, in a spirit of triangulation. Some researchers have combined different forms of data to give a new orientation to ethnographic studies: Dirksen et al. (2010), for example, describe a study which "piled on layers of understanding" by using social network analysis of log files to orient an online and offline ethnographic study of the use of a company intranet. Howard (2002) similarly describes a combination of online and offline methods, deploying social network analysis of the work of political campaign consultants to guide selection of fieldsites for ethnographic study. Online traces, such as hyperlinks, friendship connections in social networking sites, or exchange of e-mails as recorded in logs, can all lend themselves to social network analysis (Garton, Haythornthwaite, & Wellman 1997; Hogan 2008). This kind of approach can offer a stimulus to the imagination and a contextual understanding for a qualitative researcher, although, of course, a trace, for a qualitative researcher, would not be usually taken as having a singular, transparent, and objective meaning in terms of its role in a social network. As Beaulieu argues, online traces of connectivity can also offer stimulus to developing ethnography of connection (Beaulieu 2005; Beaulieu & Simakova 2006).

It has become quite commonplace for researchers to combine qualitative and quantitative approaches in Internet-based studies. Herring (2010) explored the challenge to conventional content analysis posed by the advent of blogging and proposed a novel combination of approaches to attend to its distinctive qualities. Herring et al. (2005), for example, combine social network analysis and visualization of the interconnection of blogs with a qualitative analysis of the comments between interlinked blogs. This combination of methods allows for an analysis that both exposes the "big picture" in terms of density of connections in the blog landscape and explores the micropractices of commenting and referral that help to create and sustain these patterns. Similarly, Efimova (2009) complements her rich qualitative descriptions of blogging practices with systematic visualizations of the temporal emergence of selected blog "conversations."

Some studies can blur the line between qualitative and quantitative analysis, particularly when the qualities of the Internet allow for a larger sample size than a qualitative researcher could usually achieve within an overall qualitative approach. Strano (2008) conducted an analysis of people's understanding of their Facebook profiles, concentrating on their choice of main profile image. The main body of her study focused on a survey in which people were asked open questions about how they chose their profile image and what prompted them to change it. Making the survey available online, and publicizing it widely, led to a large sample size for a qualitative study. Having asked participants to give basic demographic information in addition to their open-ended answers, Strano (2008) was able to follow up her qualitative thematic coding of answers with a statistical analysis of the extent to which particular themes were related to demographic variables.

Often, quantification is suggested to Internet researchers by the sheer amount of data available to them. Since the data are born digital, it is often relatively easy to count and compare various characteristics, and summaries of the numbers of different participants in a discussion or the rhythms of contribution become much more readily available to an online field researcher than to ethnographers in face-to-face settings, who often cannot access such detailed and comprehensive records of interaction. When these kinds of data are available, and when it is relevant to the analysis to know how many people participated, to what extent, and according to what temporal rhythms, it seems perverse not to provide a tabulation or chart to allow readers to see what is going on. Baym (2000), for example, fleshed out her careful ethnographic examination of the practices of a soap opera fan group with systematic coding of a large sample of messages according to genre and style of interaction, as well as with an analysis of posting frequencies aimed at highlighting the different roles played in the community by diverse participants. Some of these data might be quantitative, but the approach is qualitative in its ethos of a rounded understanding of practices of meaning-making.

Conventionally, quantitative approaches such as those described above might have been thought to be opposed to the contextual interpretive ethos inherent in qualitative research. Such distinctions have, however, become somewhat unfashionable in the face of recent developments in mixed-methods research (Tashakkori 2006). Even without embracing mixed methods wholeheartedly, quantification has often had some part to play within a committed qualitative approach. As Maxwell (2010) describes, there have been calls to quantify the generalizations in qualitative research (such as "some" or "often") by use of counting, and inclusion of such quantification in a qualitative piece of research can still align with overarching qualitative principles. One can quantify within an overall qualitative approach focused on a grounded understanding of practices and processes (rather than the quantitative focus on variables). For this to be so, we need, however, to be careful that the numbers we use are contextualized and meaningful within the overall qualitative understanding that we develop.

In summary, then, the following points will be helpful to keep in mind when analyzing qualitative Internet data and deciding on forms of evidence to present in research reports:

- The analytic frame that the researcher brings to a dataset does not necessarily match with the way in which participants understand what is going on here. It can be helpful to reflect on the way that a particular analytic frame has shaped both the data collected and the way in which they are interpreted. This may suggest different ways of viewing the data, or prompt a discussion of the limits to the interpretation being offered.

- Internet-derived data are often readily counted, summarized, and transformed via social network analysis or in combination with other datasets. This offers up some significant possibilities for enhancing fieldwork and data analysis, and for presenting data in forms that contextualize them and visualize relevant aspects.
- Qualitative research need not avoid counting and systematic forms of analysis altogether. These practices often enhance qualitative research writing, as long as the concepts to be quantified arise within an appropriately grounded qualitative analysis.

New Media Forms and Qualitative Writing

In addition to the possibilities for different forms of analysis, new media also offer considerable opportunities to change the format of the research report. Although the majority of academic publications are still either produced as print-on-paper or mimic the print-on-paper form in an online publication, many other formats are now possible. Dicks et al. (2005) have extensively explored the potential that new media offers for different forms of reporting on ethnography. By using hypertext,[1] they suggest that ethnographers can offer readers the chance to construct their own paths through a text, allowing the reader a greater agency to link together aspects of interest and draw his or her own conclusions. This can also be an aid to analysis, enabling the researcher to explore diverse forms of connection between data elements (Dicks & Mason, 2011). Also, new media formats offer the chance to draw much more heavily on visual materials than is usually possible in a print publication,

---

1. Hypertext is usually associated with web pages, but in fact refers to any portrayal of information in which portions of text are linked together to allow a reader to jump between them.

and to include video and audio materials. The ethnographic text can therefore present far more raw data than is usually possible for a publication and can also offer up a more evocative sense of the field by allowing readers to see and hear it, as well as read about it, depending on the affordances of different media (Dicks, Soyinka, & Coffey 2006). Of course, there is still a strong selectivity to the materials presented, and the ethnographer retains an authorial control over the pathways offered to readers through the text and the narrative that joins sections together. Nonetheless, it is clear that new media forms offer some intriguing possibilities for qualitative research reporting.

The new forms that Dicks et al. (2005) describe are by no means confined to research about the Internet: indeed, their own demonstrator example is based upon ethnography of a museum rather than a primarily digital environment (Mason & Dicks 2001). However, the kind of format that they suggest has been used to interesting effect in Internet research, particularly when researchers have built an archive of online materials and can offer readers the opportunity to navigate it for themselves. Foot and Schneider, for example, issued a "digital supplement" (http://mitpress.mit.edu/books/0262062585/WebCampaigningDigitalSupplement.html) to their book *Web Campaigning* (Foot & Schneider 2006). The book reported on their research into the use of the Internet in political campaigning in the United States. The digital supplement offered access to the full text of the book, in addition to the archive of websites upon which the analysis was based. The aim, as described by Foot and Schneider on the site itself, was as follows:

- "The Digital Supplement is designed to illustrate the text of **Web Campaigning,** beyond the ways that are possible in print, principally by giving readers access to archival impressions of the Web pages that are referenced in the book.
- It can serve as a pedagogical aid for those teaching courses about the Internet and politics. These uses may be facilitated by the downloadable version.
- The transformation of the linear text of the printed book into hypertext, along with the addition of in-context screenshots, enables different kinds of reading and sense-making practices.

- This Supplement provides an opportunity for analysts to conduct their own investigations of Web campaigning. One tool to facilitate additional analysis is the Wayfinder interface that allows visitors to tag the archived pages in this collection and build their own interpretations, on their own or in collaboration with others.
- This installation is an experiment in harnessing Web technologies to represent digital scholarship digitally. If it sparks more conversations and innovations in this important arena, the effort will be worthwhile." (Schneider, Foot, & Dougherty 2006)

Providing the digital supplement through the auspices of the publisher seems a wise move in ensuring the longevity of the resource. A resource hosted on an individual university website may be more fragile in the face of a move by the original author to a new job, a site restructuring, or a policy change on institutional web provision. It seems troubling that the gains from use of digital formats might be accompanied by a loss in terms of long-term availability of resources. Possibly, we need dedicated third-party digital archives to allow Internet researchers to provide stable and enduring access to their data. Many archives will, however, raise the kind of ethical issues already discussed in the previous chapter, in connection with reporting on digital data. Foot and Schneider's data were very clearly public, in that they focused on the campaign websites of political candidates. In other cases, it will be less clear that data are public, or at least that the data were produced in anticipation that they would be so for research purposes.

Digital supplements and online archives of research data offer ways of involving readers in the text, thus offering them the chance to navigate according to their own interests. Other forms of online reporting of qualitative research outputs offer ways of involving participants in the research process and in the writing of the research. Some researchers, indeed, have used the creation of a digital resource by and with participants as a part of conducting the research itself. Underberg describes this as part of developing a *reciprocal ethnography*, questioning "how technology can be used to build into the documentation and presentation process itself an ethnographic guide to the materials that also incorporates the particular folk group's vision of how to present these materials"

(Underberg 2006, 301). Producing a digital resource in which participants describe themselves provides a means to a deeper participation for the ethnographer, bringing the researcher's emerging perceptions into juxtaposition with participants' perceptions and concerns about how they wish to portray themselves. Forte (2005, 2006), for example, acted as webmaster for the production of online resources describing the culture and concerns of the group whom he studied, along the way finding that the production of the website actively constructed the field as much as it permitted him to study a pre-existing field (Forte 2004).

It is possible, then, to use new media resources within a piece of qualitative Internet research to transform the report, and, through this, to aim at developing new ways of engaging with participants and readers alike. This kind of innovation has the potential to blur the fieldwork boundary, including more actors in the process of interpretation and making it less of a given that the outcome will be a fixed final text—the ethnography—over which the ethnographer has authorial control. Along these lines, there has been considerable speculation that the availability of tools such as blogs could break down the traditional separation between researchers and their various audiences, and indeed, the separation between researchers and research participants. Blogs, in particular, offer an opportunity for a style of research reporting that is more timely than the traditionally slow pace of academic publishing and that makes emerging findings accessible for comment by other researchers and research participants. Whatever the potential capacities of these technologies might be to transform research processes and identities, it is still unclear to what extent those capacities will be widely taken up beyond a small number of experimenters.

Some researchers have deployed blogs as a research tool by encouraging participants to blog, as a continuation of the existing tradition of participant film in ethnography (Ward 2006). This practice offers participants the chance to produce representations of themselves through a process that may feel more empowering than a traditional interview or through being observed. Murthy (2008) suggests that the use of blogging can help to give a more prominent role in research to participants, particularly allowing the voices of those who might often be marginalized or silenced to speak. Cowan (2008), for example, describes the process of setting up a blog to encourage schoolchildren to participate in a discussion of books that they like. The blog provides for a different kind of conversation to emerge, one in which the children feel empowered to make suggestions and have opinions, and it also has effect on the real-life settings of the school library, transforming the way that they make use of it. Setting up a blog for participants can therefore be a very effective way of creating a research space over which they have some control, and the kind of self-reflection that the blog encourages can end up having a much broader impact on the research setting.

Beyond blogs as a research tool in which participants have written about themselves, many researchers have created their own blogs and written about themselves. Nancy Baym, for example, blogs about her research on online fandom (http://www.onlinefandom.com/) and on musicians' relationships with audiences (http://blog.beautifulandstrange.com/). She discusses the ongoing process of the research and addresses both readers of her published work and participants, potential and actual, in the ongoing research. The blog thus becomes a work-in-progress that situates Baym in the field as much as she is commenting on the field. Philip Budka maintains a blog (http://www.philbu.net/blog/) reflecting on his ethnographic fieldwork on a group of indigenous Canadians' use of the Internet, as well as discussing the development of anthropological knowledge of and in new media. He also maintains a research website that is addressed to a wide audience of research participants and potential readers, as the front page explains:

> This meeting place webpage provides **information about research projects** on MyKnet.org. It also should **get people together** who are interested in MyKnet.org and who are using MyKnet.org as homepage producers and users. (Budka n.d.)

By juxtaposing these various audiences and stages of the research process, Budka's work effectively blurs the boundary between ethnography as process and ethnography as product, making clear that the researcher's engagement is ongoing and the interpretive work always, in some sense, unfinished. He also provides a space for participant voices to develop alongside that of the ethnographer.

Efimova's research on the blogging practices of knowledge workers posed her an enormous reflexive challenge since she both began the research as a blogger herself and continued to blog throughout the research, about the research. She wrestled with the extent to which her blogging practices should inform or be present within the final thesis that she prepared and also with the extent to which her own blogging about blogging would impact on the bloggers whom she studied:

> As I blogged on the progress of my research, other bloggers could easily follow those posts, creating influences and feedback loops that researchers usually learn to avoid in order to escape 'contaminating their data.' (Efimova 2009, 31)

She describes the role conflicts that she experiences and discusses agonizing over whether to comment on emerging blog conversations she feels drawn to on the blogs themselves as an ordinary blogger might, or whether to leave the blogs uncontaminated and use them as data to analyze for her thesis.

Wakeford and Cohen (2008) capture the tensions that researchers experience in deciding how much of the research process to reveal in a blog by describing blogs as "fieldnotes in public." Traditionally, the researcher's fieldnotes have been a private affair, only selectively revealed to evidence a specific line of argument in a tidied-up report prepared for public viewing. The blog as a form of public discourse that presents the thoughts of the researcher in a stream of small, frequent interventions in some ways mirrors the role of fieldnotes, but also deviates from standard practice, since the fieldnote is not usually for public consumption. The introduction of blogging into research practice challenges the taken-for-granted status of fieldnotes as the private working notes of the researcher. Cohen's postings to his blog about his research on photobloggers thus include descriptions of interviews he has just conducted, thoughts about emergent themes and possible analytic directions to pursue, and reflections on theoretical resources, which might otherwise have had a purely private existence (Wakeford & Cohen 2008).

Blogging can also cast into doubt the researcher's singular role as author of the written text, since blogs allow for comments and challenges to appear alongside the original post and hence can have a collaborative, emergent quality. This potentially allows for what Gregg (2006) describes as *conversational scholarship* to emerge, but

as Cohen (Wakeford & Cohen 2008) describes, although others
have had some success with this strategy, he found that it was necessary to turn off the commenting feature as his blog became a tar-
get for spam. As Wakeford and Cohen (2008) describe, the nature
of blogging is evolving, and whatever effects blogging might have
are not determined by the technology itself but rather are the outcome of conventions of practice that could have been otherwise.
They are, therefore, cautious about claims that use of blogging
drives us toward a new form of scholarship, reshaping the publics
for academic discourse (Halavais 2006).

In an age when researchers are judged by their productivity,
and where the status of outlets such as journals is often crucial in
judging the worth of research outputs, it is possibly not surprising
that there are still relatively few researchers who blog prolifically.
When it is not directly connected to a form of quality-assured output, it can be difficult to justify the input of time and the intellec-
tual commitment to keep a research blog alive. Nonetheless, the
examples described above show that some researchers have found
them to be a highly effective methodological tool, impacting on
both the research process and the resulting research report (which
remains, however, very often produced in conventional format).
The use of blogs can also be a principled response to the usual
"cleaning-up" process that goes on when we shift from research
as an activity to research output: some researchers use blogging to
"make the ordinary visible" (Oulasvirta, Lehtonen, Kurvinen, &
Raento 2010), revealing aspects of the contingent, emergent qualities of research.

It is difficult to make an assessment of the extent to which blogging has been adopted as academic practice that would be more
than a guess. Although attempts have been made to survey blogging communities, it can be complicated to locate relevant blogs,
and samples and surveys are thus often incomplete (Li & Walejko
2008). Henry Farrell's listing of academic blogs (http://www.aca-
demicblogs.org/) certainly contains many vibrant and insightful
blogs, but it likely that these are still very much a minority form of
academic practice. They are also quite diverse in style: there is no
single way to blog as an academic. Bukvova et al. (2010) explored
the uses that researchers were making of blogs, using a qualitative
approach to focus on the blogs of German social and natural scientists in particular. The sample included only researchers who were

heavily engaged in online communications, which the researchers operationalized as meaning that they both blogged and made use of Twitter. The participants were asked for their permission to analyze their blog posts, and when consent was not forthcoming, their data were excluded from the study. Although the study thus ultimately only looked at a small sample of bloggers, it was evident that patterns of blog use varied widely, both in terms of the kind of content researchers included and the extent to which they made their blog into a personal platform.

Beyond the blog as a (mainly) single-authored space into which others can insert comments, *wikis* extend the collaborative model yet further. A wiki acts as a space on the Internet in which any authorized contributor can add material, delete material, or edit existing contributions (this facility may be password protected but need not necessarily be so). The wiki thus acts as a collaboratively produced resource, with the collaboratively authored open-access encyclopedia Wikipedia (http://www.wikipedia.org) being the best known. Wikis have been used extensively within educational settings, particularly supporting student projects and allowing for group engagement and reflection on learning experiences (Cummings & Barton 2008). It is also possible to use a wiki to support a collaborative research project, developing a shared writing space in which researchers can work together to add resources and build on one another's interpretations (Schroeder & Besten 2008; Anandarajan & Anandarajan 2010; Fitzgerald & Findlay, 2011). Many academic wikis act as shared spaces to map out a field or provide a guide to resources. Qualitative Internet researchers could certainly use a wiki to present a collaborative environment that would allow participants to add their contributions and view one another's input. The Creative Climate online resource (http://www.open.ac.uk/openlearn/nature-environment/the-environment/creative-climate), created by Joe Smith of the Open University, contains numerous responses to the issues of climate change in the form of online diaries, which readers can rate and comment upon. However, a review of the landscape of scholarly wikis and other "virtual research environments" concludes that there are diverse formats, but that encouraging participation and ensuring sustainability are often problematic (Carusi & Reimer 2010).

While discussing research uses of Web 2.0-style emergent scholarly resources, it is also worth mentioning micro-blogging.

The most popular of the micro-blogging services is Twitter, which allows users to post brief comments (140 characters or less) that will be seen by those who have chosen to subscribe to (follow) their output. Interesting or useful material will often be "retweeted" to a reader's own set of followers, thus facilitating a viral spread of messages across a network of connected followers who may be far removed from the initiator of the message. It is not, however, inevitable that Twitter use will be public, and some users restrict their messages to a known group of recipients. Messages related to the same topic can be rendered viewable as a collection if they all include the same *hashtag* (a word to indicate the topic prefaced by #).

Twitter has developed a following in academic circles, but (perhaps not surprisingly given the difficulty of compressing a complex message into 140 characters or less) it is more used for talk about research or for sharing useful references than for disseminating the results of research itself. In particular, Twitter has become an accompaniment to many academic conferences (Letierce, Passant, Breslin, & Decker 2010a). Participants will post messages about the progress of the conference and of the paper presentations they are attending, offering a real-time online reflection on the offline events. These conference-related *tweets* tend to be directed within the community of people already at the conference or directly interested in a particular field of work (Letierce, Passant, Breslin, & Decker 2010b), and they will often have limited relevance for nonparticipants (Ebner et al. 2010). Although everyday use of Twitter is often dismissed by commentators as essentially trivial, for the participants concerned here, this particular use of Twitter is seen as a part of academic practice. Priem and Costello (2010) study the content of academic Twitter use and find that mentions of academic work in tweets can be seen as analogous to citations. These Twitter citations happen very quickly, as part of a conversation, and are valued in that they present a recommendation of something to read from someone else in the field.

This survey of various ways in which new media can be used in reporting qualitative Internet research must inevitably be a snapshot in time, discussing those technologies prevalent at the time of writing. New forms may be just around the corner, and some thoroughly entrenched technologies of today may soon be yesterday's news. This is a sobering thought for any academic who likes to think that her words will be read in years to come. For purposes of posterity, print on paper has yet to be beaten as the academic medium of choice. Nonetheless, the technologies available today have been used by some pioneering researchers, as described above, and found to have some interesting methodological advantages, as well as posing new challenges. In summary, the current possibilities described in this section include:

- Producing the qualitative research report in a hypermedia format that includes raw data in diverse media and offers readers multiple routes through the text
- Providing an archived resource that allows readers to navigate the raw data on which a text is based, such as an archive of websites
- Developing reciprocal ethnography, working with participants to create a digital resource as part of the research process
- Encouraging visibility of participants' voices by providing them with a blog or wiki to share their thoughts
- Blogging the researcher's emerging thoughts to open up the research process to a wider audience
- Developing a "virtual research environment" or collaborative workspace using a wiki that can be readily updated by all participants in a project
- Using micro-blogging to develop scholarly conversations and share thoughts and resources in real-time.

Summary
Breaking Out of the Traditional Narrative

The examples discussed in this chapter show that qualitative Internet researchers need not stay within the confines of traditional approaches to analyzing and reporting on research. There are multiple possibilities for blending different media and data sources, for developing different reporting formats, and for engaging research participants and readers in new ways. The advent of scholarship 2.0 has been predicted as a radical reworking of the conditions of knowledge production and the status of the academy. Still, however, researchers tend to be quite conservative, and actual uptake of Web 2.0 for research reporting is quite rare (Maynard & O'Brien 2010). Some of the following concerns may prompt qualitative researchers to stay with more traditional forms of research report.

Leaving Behind the Security of an Uncontaminated Field

Many of the currently popular forms of Internet communication are openly accessible to a broad public, in practice if not in principle. Although it is possible to restrict an online communication such as a website or blog to a known audience, it is not conventional to use them in this way, and most users appreciate the ability of the Internet to open up communications to an audience that they cannot predict in advance. Doing so, however, can mean that those aspects of the research process that are usually held private, such as the researchers' fieldnotes, begin to circulate publicly among the research participants. Such forms of Internet communication, then, flout the researcher's instinct to study the field without having an undue influence upon it. Of course, the researcher always did impact on the field simply by being there, but the unrestricted sharing of emerging research themes and interpretations via a blog takes this contamination to a new level, and we have little experience of what the consequences of such sharing might be for the research.

Opening up Our Interpretations to be Contradicted or Appropriated

Research is always open to comment, contradiction, or appropriation in so far as we make it publicly available. We then hope that it will be used and cited by other researchers and accept that those citations will often enter into debate with the conclusions that we have drawn. This appropriation generally happens, however, within a community that shares certain agreed standards for how research should be judged and what form it is appropriate for debates to take. When materials are made publicly available on the Internet, and when the format invites comment without requiring the membership of a particular interpretive community, the responses may not be what researchers are used to. Responses from outside an interpretive community can be dismissive, hostile, or simply seem inappropriate to the researcher. When the research is taken up and used, these uses can be surprising and take liberties with the researchers' idea of what their contributions might be.

Leaving the Certainty of a Finished Research Product

There is a rhythm to much of our research experience, with the time space of projects determined by funding availability or by the expected duration of graduate registration. We routinely carve up research into periods of preparation, fieldwork, write-up, and publication, and we see the final publication as an end point to the process. Even though our research agenda spills over from one project to another, and the concerns from one project will inform another that succeeds or runs alongside it, we find security in having finished a project and being able to point to the product that resulted. By contrast, many contemporary Internet applications embrace an unfinished quality that makes them always work in progress, never to be thought of as closed and complete. Digital resources resist closure. This unfinished quality can be a challenge to the researcher's sense of achievement in a project and also a difficult concept to promote in a research evaluation environment that values finished products.

Stepping Outside the Comfortable Boundaries of Research Precedents and Agreed Standards of Quality

Although quality in research is never easy to define, it is, at least, an emergent property judged by a community of peers, through such mechanisms as the examination process for Ph.D. theses and the peer review of journal articles. We go through a period of apprenticeship to a discipline, often as an undergraduate, then as a Ph.D. student, in which we learn the skills and values of our field. Judgments of quality in research practice depend heavily on precedent and on fitting in with the accepted practices of a particular interpretive community of like-minded researchers. For this reason, innovation in research practice, whether it be a new way of collecting data, a new form of analysis, or a different way of reporting on research, can be problematic. When we step outside the comfortable boundaries of research precedents, it becomes harder for the value of what we have done to be judged according to agreed-upon standards. It is vital for research practice to innovate and move with the times, but often the developments are incremental and will involve carefully demonstrating their continuity with established principles involved in new forms of practice. Internet research has, indeed, showed a balance of innovation and continuity with past principles throughout its history (Hine 2005).

Transgressing Expectations of Publishers, Universities, Research Sponsors

When a researcher wishes to explore a new form of research output, there will often be resistance, or at the very least caution, from publishers, from an employing university, and from research sponsors. Publishers have vested interests in the established system and will be concerned to see that these interests are not contravened by new forms of output. To be sure, a researcher is free to innovate, but when he or she wishes to publish a conventional monograph or journal article alongside a digital resource, the publisher may be understandably cautious to assess whether the digital resource is competing with the conventional output. Employing universities and research sponsors tend to be conservative in their approach to the quality of research outlets, although open-access publishing has been latterly embraced by funding bodies keen to ensure that researchers make their work as widely available as possible. Conventional publishing systems carry the danger that research is paid for twice, once for the funding of the researcher who produces it and again through subscriptions that enable other researchers to read it. There are many stakeholders in the research process, and their concerns may pull the researcher in different directions when innovative practices are concerned. Online open-access research publishing has the potential to meet some concerns of research sponsors, but threatens the business model of conventional academic publishing and also requires creative approaches to quality assurance.

Facing up to Audience Inertia

Recent years have seen numerous experiments in opening up academic debate and widening access to scholarship via online environments. Many of the initiatives that require academic researchers to invest time in publicly commenting on the research of others and debating their interpretations have found it difficult to recruit sufficient interest to be sustainable. There is considerable audience inertia and caution in the face of new forms of the debating arena, and there may be a resistance to making an investment of time in a new activity that has yet to achieve mainstream status. There are, to be sure, some committed communities of academic bloggers and micro-bloggers, but many researchers simply feel that they lack the time to invest in yet one more means of communication.

It seems, then, that there are massive obstacles to a widespread uptake of various forms of new media-related research practice. This applies to qualitative Internet researchers as much as to any other researchers, since they still depend on the academic publishing system, participate in interpretive communities, are judged by peers, and are employed by universities and other research establishments. There remain, however, many benefits to developing these new forms of practice, and for a creative researcher with the courage to face up to some of the obstacles, these can be seized upon. Among the benefits for a qualitative Internet researcher interested in developing innovative reporting practices are the following:

New Engagements with Research Participants

One of the most appealing prospects of Internet-assisted forms of research reporting is that they potentially open our work up to new audiences. It is more appealing to think of one's words being available to whoever wants to read them than to think of them locked away in a subscription-only journal of limited circulation or contained in a printed thesis of which only two copies exist in a university library somewhere. The Internet makes it possible to publish a research report that could be read without these kinds of restriction on circulation. Some forms of Internet publishing promise something more radical, however. By making research more accessible, and by opening up the research process as well as the research product to wider audiences, new forms of Internet-assisted research writing offer to bring participants into the research process and the research report in a more active fashion. The concern that the research process sets up a boundary between researchers and researched, with a disempowering effect on the ability of those being researched to tell their own story, has long been prevalent in qualitative research. These new forms of reporting on research process and outcomes offer some very practical ways of breaking down that boundary and conducting new forms of participatory and collaborative research.

New Ways of Doing Research as Teams

In addition to the possibility of engaging research participants in a more active fashion, Internet-assisted research reporting also offers the prospect of more collaboration between teams of researchers. It can often be difficult to organize work as a team so that collective analysis of large datasets can be done. Virtual research environments offer the prospect of allowing teams of researchers to work together while apart, to carry out analysis together and to develop shared resources, thus supporting the kind of activity that Sudweeks and Rafaeli (1996) describe occurring in ProjectH, a computer-mediated collaborative effort to collect and conduct content analysis on a large sample of discussion list messages.

New Ways of Making Evocative Accounts

New media forms of reporting for qualitative research help us to move outside the confines of text. Offering up more data, in different formats and media, and developing innovative ways of analyzing, quantifying, and visualizing these data help us to see our field in new ways and present it to audience in a more evocative fashion. When we want audiences to understand how we experienced the field and offer them the chance to feel that they know how it was to be there, these additional forms of representation can be a great asset.

Innovative Ways of Incorporating Reflexivity into Our Work

One final aspect of Internet-assisted research reporting of key significance to the qualitative researcher is the prospect of an enhanced presence of reflexivity in the text. By moving away from a final research report that presents a single authorial narrative analysis and into a data-enriched hypertextual report that openly invites the reader to juxtapose his own analysis and find his own path through it, we may be able to increase consciousness of the contingency of interpretation. Making fieldnotes into public documents via blogging also offers to increase the presence of the researcher in the text, and interactive formats encourage the researcher to face up to the prospect of alternative interpretations.

There are, then, considerable potential benefits for qualitative Internet researchers able to embrace new forms of research reporting, although how important these are to any particular researcher and any specific research project will vary. The particular qualities of Internet-derived qualitative data as born-digital and the sheer extent of the data so often available prompt researchers to explore the possibilities that the Internet provides for their own research. It remains to be seen, however, whether the principled objections and infrastructural sources of inertia can be overcome sufficiently for many of these innovative practices to become mainstream. In the final chapter, I reflect on the extent to which qualitative research practice has so far been transformed with the advent of the Internet, reflect on the consequences for our evaluation of qualitative Internet research reports, and speculate on what might be to come.

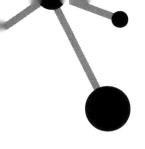

5

EVALUATING AND LOOKING TO THE FUTURE

Particular mundane technologies may well be talked about and referred to in various economies and in society at large (e.g. through other media), but the technologies themselves are rarely the focus of the talk when in use. We can argue that, at least when fully operational, in making action and interactions visible and available these technologies have themselves disappeared. The argument we make then is that the use and display of these technologies, in them becoming mundane, has become less important than the display and engagement of the self that they support.

—Dourish, Graham, Randall, &
Rouncefield, 2010, p. 177

The writing of this book has inevitably intruded on family life along the way, and quite a large proportion has been written at weekends when my children were around. It was therefore not unreasonable that my 8-year-old daughter should ask, after several weekends when I had been distracted by writing, what the book was about. She knows broadly that my interest in sociology involves finding out about what people do, so I told her that the book was about how we should go about finding out what people do by using the Internet. She looked straight at me and, without missing a beat, said "I know that. You'd go on Facebook and ask them. Or you'd e-mail them and write back and forth to find out." She paused, and smiled. "Or, I know one you won't think of, you'd go on Club Penguin and see." It was, to her, completely obvious that if you wanted to know about what people did, you would go to the Internet to find them. She used a natural methodological imagination to dream up ways of finding out about people using the Internet, using what, for her, was a mundane technology (Dourish et al. 2010). None of our prevailing anxieties about the quality of data you would gain from Internet interactions, the authenticity of identities, or the ethics of online research troubled her. It was simply obvious that you would go to where people hung out online and ask them.

The Internet for an 8-year-old is, thankfully, still a fairly innocent place, and none of the more complex adult aspects of its use has yet come into view. There are, indeed, many reasons why you cannot simply go online and ask people what they do, as my daughter suggested. Still, her acceptance of the obviousness of online interactions as a means to find out about people is quite telling. Much of the agonizing that still goes on about whether qualitative research using the Internet is desirable or adequate is based on a premise that Internet interactions could not possibly live up to the qualities of face-to-face interactions. It is time to realize that there is now a generation for whom using the Internet may be an obvious, sensible, unproblematic thing to do, and the old debates about whether the Internet is, in itself, good enough for qualitative research may have been overtaken by events.

Given the increasing mundanity of the Internet and the proliferation of research-relevant applications that it offers, this concluding chapter considers the current status of qualitative Internet research in social research and explores its future prospects. The next section looks at how far research itself has been transformed with the advent of the Internet and questions how far fundamental principles have stayed the same. A section on the evaluation of Internet research then suggests a series of questions to ask of Internet research studies, focusing on conventional criteria used in evaluating qualitative research. The chapter then concludes with a section on the future prospects for qualitative Internet research.

We face the potential for further integration of qualitative Internet research with different forms of data synthesis and mining. There is a prospect of using Web 2.0 technologies more extensively within the research process to break down boundaries between production and consumption of research. The increasingly pervasive use of mobile and personal technologies poses some quite difficult challenges to the commitment of qualitative research to in-depth understanding. Facing up to these issues is going to involve a continued careful reflection on what it is that qualitative research hopes to achieve and requires some agile methodological thinking to adapt our research and writing to new situations.

Social Science and the Internet

A set of videos widely available on the Internet showcases the vision of the Knowledge Navigator, conceived for Apple by John Sculley in 1987 (Sculley 1987). In my particularly favorite video, an academic walks into his home office, takes off his jacket, and begins to chat with his computer. In natural conversational style, he interacts with the humanoid virtual personal assistant (somewhat bizarrely clad in shirt and bow-tie) who appears on the screen, checking his messages and diary, finding articles he wants to read, and talking by video-link with a distant colleague. The assistant copes miraculously with ill-specified and ambiguous requests, finding the required information when given just a few vague clues, displaying complex simulations, and assessing correlations on demand. For the academic in this video, the Knowledge Navigator allows him seamless access to his field of research, which is deforestation. The computer acts as an extension of his memory, retrieving for him things that he hazily knows but cannot specifically call to mind, and anticipating his wants with things he does not even know yet that he needs. The Knowledge Navigator allows the researcher to inhabit his field of research.

Sculley's vision from 1987 has, of course, not been entirely realized. Although many components of the system depicted in the video have become commonplace, the ease of interaction and the ability of the computer to interpret natural language (and correctly guess the user's intentions) remain far from realistic. I can approximate something of the computer's substitution of clever searching and retrieval for actual clear memories when I use repeated Google searches on half-remembered connections to try and locate a paper that I vaguely recall having read but for which I cannot remember either the author or the title with any exactitude. It would be nice to have some artificial intelligence to do this for me, but I doubt if it could ever reproduce the bizarre connections my faulty memory sometimes makes to come up with the right answer. There are, though, now some knowledge navigation systems aimed at supporting the research process that do some of this work. E-science researchers have developed various forms of collaboratory and work-flow support systems for particular communities (Hey & Trefethen 2002; Yang, Wang, & Jie 2011). For a wider constituency, Mendeley (https://www.mendeley.com) now offers something a little like the Knowledge Navigator's awareness of a field of literature, together with a kind of social networking support not readily envisaged in 1987, although without a link to raw data.

Viewing the Knowledge Navigator video now, and reflecting on how unattainable it seemed at the time and how many of its features have actually come to pass, gives me pause for thought at the extent to which our work itself may have changed. Our awareness of fields of academic knowledge is increasingly shaped by the various technologies that suffuse and mediate access to them, and it is interesting to reflect on what this does to the knowledge that we produce. In recent years, the Internet has transformed the practice of research, if not always in directions that we might have expected or can easily articulate. Some of these transformations are common to many fields of academic research, whereas others are confined to specific research communities. From the initiation of a research project through to the completion of a publishable manuscript, our practices have become increasingly dependent on information and communication technologies. When we say that we search or browse the literature, we generally now mean that we search databases, follow links, and click on promising leads. Our computers do not read our minds in the way that Sculley's Knowledge Navigator did, but various kinds of serendipity and search algorithms combined shape what we see.

Some of the new computer-mediated academic practices are specific to particular modes of analysis. Although e-science and cyberinfrastructures have received much attention as means to increase the scale and efficiency of research practice in the sciences (Yang et al. 2011), there have also been somewhat less publicized, but still significant changes in how social scientists work. As a qualitative researcher, I used to work with swathes of printout, color-coded, cut up and pasted onto index cards, painstakingly ordered and rearranged in physical space as new concepts emerged. Increasingly, those data have moved into computer memory and are navigated by computer-aided qualitative data analysis (CAQDAS) packages that store my codes and allow me to reorder fragments in virtual space as my concepts emerge (Lewins & Silver 2007). Are they, I wonder, the same concepts as those I would have arrived at "by hand"? Are they different? Could they even be better? And have I lost anything in the move away from hand-crafted analysis?

When we say that we "write," in fact we often now compose texts on a computer screen, typing in sections, editing them and moving them around to best effect, calling up references as we write from personal databases of relevant literature and online sources that constantly link us forward to fields we didn't already know about. Although many of us still write conventional dissertations and theses, and draft academic papers to be published in printed journals, we can also use their open-access online counterparts, and we can blog, tweet, and work in hypertext. Each mode of communication has a potential impact on what it is that can be said, just as the original shift from orality to literacy impacted on what knowledge could be (Ong 1982). The mundane technologies of knowledge production potentially have a significant impact on the nature of knowledge itself. Dourish et al. (2010) describe the processes through which, in becoming a mundane part of our lives, a technology fades from view, so that we become less and less conscious of the part it plays in making particular actions possible. It is important, then, to pause to reflect on the extent to which the Internet could, or indeed should, become a mundane technology in qualitative research. What might we be gaining, and what might we lose in the process? ✦

The ways that academic writers explore fields of knowledge, communicate with colleagues, analyze their data, and write up the results have changed incrementally yet radically with the increasing normalization and creeping functionality of computers in our working practices, and they have the potential to change yet further (Dutton & Jeffreys 2010). For social scientists, however, there has been an additional transformation to contend with. The fabric of social life itself has been undergoing a transformation with the advent of new forms of media and interpersonal communication, and this transformation has posed new challenges and provided significant opportunities for our research practice. For social scientists, there has thus been a real shift in the very object that we study. Recent advances in technology seem sometimes to have moved faster than we can keep up with (Beer & Burrows 2007), as new forms of social interaction and presence have developed on the Internet. Going back to the academic studying deforestation in the Knowledge Navigator video, although the way in which he explored his field of research had changed, at least his research object itself was still out there in the world in the same way as before. As a social scientist interested in how people live meaningful and organized lives, I have had to recognize that a significant amount of that living now goes on through various forms of mediated interaction. The research object for a social scientist has undergone a significant shift in the time since the making of the Knowledge Navigator video. Given this shift, the question is: What has changed and what still stays the same in our research principles and practice?

By accepting the Internet as a mundane part of qualitative social research and accepting that what people do there has to be taken seriously as much as what they do anywhere else, I would argue that our research practice is adapting to the prevailing conditions, as it must do in order to survive and remain relevant. Our research practices need to follow where the people are and take account of what it is that they do. However, the question of what might be lost in the process is still a very pertinent one. Although people do live aspects of their lives online, they do not live entire lives there, and the face-to-face interactions of everyday life remain hugely important. Moving qualitative research online should not, then, entail an unthinking abandonment of the face-to-face, just because using the Internet is more convenient, cheaper, and more accessible. Instead, the advent of the new technology can offer up a very useful reflexive moment that prompts us to think about what it is that we value in our research practices and what are the fundamental values that underpin them. To this end, I move, in the next section, to discuss in a bit more detail what quality criteria we might apply to evaluating qualitative Internet research. If research practices are changing, then it is useful to think about the way that we might judge whether they are good or bad. This enables us to explore the extent to which, even though the Internet offers new fieldsites and new forms of data, the quality criteria by which the research is evaluated remain recognizably the same as for the more established forms of qualitative research.

Evaluating Qualitative Internet Research

There has been extensive discussion of the different criteria we might use for judging the quality of various forms of research. In each case, the criteria capture reasons why we might treat a particular piece of research as a viable representation of some aspect of the world around us, upon which we might then base further research, policies, or practical actions. Traditionally, quantitative research is expected to display qualities of validity, reliability, replicability, and generalizability. Since qualitative research is based on very different principles to quantitative research, it is no surprise that ways of judging its quality differ. Lincoln and Guba (1985) offer criteria of credibility, transferability, dependability, and confirmability as an alternative, based on the principles to which the qualitative researcher subscribes. Subsequently, Guba and Lincoln (1989) added in consideration of the various forms of authenticity to which qualitative research might subscribe, given that the interpretivist research tradition does not accept a notion of a singular underlying reality that research can reveal. Seale discusses the development of a "criteriology" over the years, based upon different qualitative research traditions, which has ultimately led, he suggests, to a "mass of conflicting positions" (Seale 1999, 466) faced by the practicing researcher trying to predict the criteria by which his or her work might be judged. Seale proposes a pragmatic path through the complexity of criteria for qualitative research, suggesting that we can usefully draw on the criteria used in many different research traditions to help us to reflect on what might make our own research better.

In that spirit of pragmatic use of criteria from different traditions, I offer here a set of questions to ask about a piece of qualitative Internet research writing in order to help us to decide how good it is (taking "good" as a very broad-based quality judgment that will inevitably translate in different ways for our own circumstances).

As Bryman et al. (2008) suggest, practicing researchers in different fields may differ quite markedly in the quality criteria they habitually use, and their criteria may in turn differ substantially from the formal lists of criteria that the methodological texts prescribe. The questions I offer here are deliberately broad, and the extent to which they apply to different research traditions and circumstances will vary depending, for example, on whether the product being judged is an undergraduate dissertation intended as an "apprentice piece" to display research skills or is a practically oriented piece of commissioned research intended to change the way professionals do their jobs. Here, then, is a set of general concerns that may be applicable:

Can I Tell Clearly What the Researcher Did and What Limits There Are on the Study?

In line with the "transparency" criterion that researchers often apply (Bryman et al. 2008), it is important to be able to tell exactly what a researcher did to generate and analyze his or her data. In Internet research, there are many important points on which a researcher might be vague, and these can be quite significant for the extent to which we trust the results and can feel confident in applying them to other situations. For example, we may want to know how respondents were recruited because a self-selecting sample of people who happen to respond to an appeal on a public forum may be very different from a carefully identified set of interviewees found through personal connections. This does not mean that the former is uninteresting, but we need to know which we are dealing with.

Was the Research Population Appropriate to the Question and Did Use of Internet Methods Impose Unacceptable or Unacknowledged Biases?

Once we are clear about what the researcher did, we are then in a position to assess whether an appropriate research population were recruited in order to allow the specific research question that the researcher was asking to be answered. We can then go on to ask ourselves how far the questions that we bring to our reading of the report align with the actual question the original researcher asked.

It might be that he or she recruited a suitable population for a very carefully defined question, but asking the question in a slightly different way would require a different set of respondents. It is particularly important when research populations are recruited via the Internet to ask ourselves whether this introduced any undesirable or unacknowledged biases into the research population. Does it matter for the scope of the findings, for example, if only people who were active contributors to a forum were included in the study, rather than those who read without contributing? What difference does it make to our use of the findings if the research population are systematically biased toward higher income, more formally educated people, as Internet users still tend to be?

Was the Medium of Interaction Appropriate to the Population and the Topic?

If computer-mediated communications of some kind are used to interact with participants, we may need to ask how comfortable it was for that specific population, and also how suitable it was for a particular topic. Was the medium chosen for the convenience of the researcher? Or, were there specific features that were a benefit, such as the use of visual anonymity to allow participants to feel safer in discussing a sensitive topic, or use of an asynchronous medium to allow a busy population a chance to take part? If a goal of qualitative research is often to put participants at their ease and encourage them to talk in their own terms as naturally as possible, can we be convinced that the specific medium chosen enabled this to happen?

Are the Interpretations Plausible and Do They Feel Authentic in Light of the Particular Qualities of Internet Data?

A criterion for judging qualitative research identified by Lincoln and Guba (1985) is its credibility. Just as with other forms of qualitative research, we will often want to judge qualitative Internet research by how readily we believe the researcher's interpretations of what is going on. We will want to feel that we have been presented with a clear enough description, and enough of the data, to feel that we understand the setting. We will also want to be convinced when we read the researchers' interpretations of these data that they shed novel light on it, but in a way that fits in plausibly with what we already know. When qualitative research data is derived from use of the Internet, the results will need to be plausible in terms of what we already know about the topic from other settings. It may be that quite different findings will emerge from Internet research contexts, but, at the very least, the gaps need to be identified and accounted for. For example, when we find that people in anonymous online settings have free and frank exchanges on sexual health, which differ markedly from the way they speak in face-to-face contexts, we may go on to make use of the Internet-derived data, but we need first to identify and account for the differences, based on the taboos that usually surround this kind of talk between strangers face-to-face.

Has the Analysis Been Presented to the Participants, and What Was Their Response?

Lincoln and Guba (1985) identify member-checking as one of the key aspects of establishing credibility. If the people on whom the research is based consider it plausible and consider that it sheds novel but convincing light on their situation, then our confidence in the researcher's interpretations will be increased. Of course, this becomes a problematic criterion to apply if we take it to mean that qualitative researchers can only say things that are immediately recognizable to the research participants. Member-checking may not be applicable to all situations, and the process of discussing research findings with members is subject to many biases, limitations in transparency, and possibilities for being shaped by circumstance, just like any other research encounter. Nonetheless, particularly in Internet research, when qualitative researchers may be tempted to collect archival data, conduct covert research, and make interpretations without interacting with participants, some form of member-checking can be very useful in giving us more confidence in interpretations. Indeed, recruiting a research population via the Internet can mean that member-checking is made considerably easier, since draft copies of reports can be e-mailed or uploaded to websites and feedback sought electronically. A wide variety of interactive forums for the researched to speak back to researchers become possible.

Is the Research Well-Founded on Existing Knowledge Going Beyond the Specifics of a Particular Internet Situation? Is the Contribution to Existing Knowledge Clearly Articulated?

I have discussed earlier a concern that qualitative Internet research should not be written as if it only applies to a very specific online context. This feeds into Lincoln and Guba's (1985) concern with the transferability of qualitative research, focused on the extent to which we can make a piece of in-depth research with one focus speak to other areas of concern. When research is focused on the Internet, it is important to make clear just how this very specific site speaks to wider concerns of interest. If a piece of Internet-based qualitative research only refers to literature focused on the Internet, I would be worried about its transferability and also concerned about the quality of the analysis, since it would appear that the author had closed off his or her mind to the contribution that the heritage of his or her discipline could offer. It is a mistake to think of the Internet as always incontrovertibly new and different from what has gone before.

Is There a Methodologically Defensible Reason Why Internet-Mediated Interaction Was Deployed?

A final criterion that folds many of the preceding concerns together is that the use of the Internet for qualitative research needs to be a methodologically defensible decision, made because we find that it offers some specific advantage as a means of researching some aspect of contemporary social life of significance beyond mere curiosity. It is not sufficient to conduct research out of idle curiosity: we need to feel that the researcher is engaged in a purposive activity as part of an academic project to contribute to knowledge, and, in this sense, our assessment of qualitative Internet research should be on its results, where it proves itself a useful, believable means to explore significant aspects of contemporary life in line with our methodological principles.

The criteria for evaluating research do not, therefore, change markedly when the research is conducted via the Internet. The principles stay broadly the same, even though some of the practical challenges are new, and really high-quality Internet research will tell us something significant about how the contemporary world is organized and experienced. It will do so if we are able to show that we are making use of the Internet not just because it is convenient, or because we didn't have the funding for face-to-face interviews, but because it offers a way to reach a particular set of people and to understand their concerns in a satisfactory way.

As the development of mobile and personal communications and the embedding of Internet media in everyday life continues to expand, the situations that are on offer to study are ever more complex, and continual challenges are posed to our methodological imaginations. High-quality qualitative research that seeks to understand contemporary life has to grapple with the Internet as a conduit through which life is lived. It also has to contend with the challenging opportunities that the Internet offers as a means through which research is carried out and reported. Some of these opportunities change the format of research and blur the boundaries of academic research itself in some interesting ways. The ability of the Internet to make data available and searchable in abundance, and the possibilities it offers for new and enhanced forms of engagement with research participants throughout the life cycle of a project can make us feel that everything has changed. It is still important, however, to reflect on what it is that counts as good research within the specific set of circumstances that we experience, and to try to make sure that whatever changes we enact are directed toward making research better.

Qualitative Internet Research 2.0, 3.0, and Beyond...

I am reluctant to predict what the future of qualitative Internet research might be because, to a large extent, this depends on what the future of the Internet might be. The development of the Internet thus far has been a heady mix of self-fulfilling prophecy, people-power, capitalism, anarchy, and complete surprises, and there is no reason to think that the future is any more easily read. There are, however, some interesting challenges on the near-horizon, based on the Internet we already have. If some of the recent developments in commercial Internet applications and everyday Internet use gain more uptake in academic circles, then the landscape of academic research broadly, and qualitative Internet research in particular, could be subject to some significant transformations.

These changes could affect both the role of the researcher as expert analyst and the nature of the social reality that we seek to explore. For a qualitative researcher, one of the key features of the Internet is the unaccustomed abundance of data that it offers, combined with a lack of tools to cope with this abundance. The increase in born-digital data suggests that moves toward more use of qualitative research tools that organize, code, and systematically explore that data could seem increasingly desirable. We may yet see qualitative researchers more broadly accepting the possibility that various forms of automatic coding, data-mining, and visualization could inform their work, using a rationale initially based simply on the increased possibility of dealing with qualitative data on a large scale, but building in momentum as results begin to accrue and the research proves itself in scope and significance. According to the principles of qualitative research, this move away from the interpretations of the embodied researcher seems problematic, but it may prove difficult to resist. One of the key concerns that arises in the face of this wealth of data is the risk that we quickly forget what we lose by only analyzing that which is available in online archives. We will need to hold quite strongly to the need to contextualize data, according to whatever forms of context become significant in the situations that concern us, and not to accept the prior availability of data as a taken-for-granted way to define a study.

Some of the changes on the horizon focus on the potential of the Internet to break down boundaries between the consumption and production of research, and between researcher and researched. Already, the products of academic research are more widely available to a general readership than ever before: the more we publish in open access outlets, the more we make our work available to anyone who might wish to read it, whether they belong to our own interpretive community or not. Various forms of research blogging, interactive resource, and participatory research space challenge the idea of research as a process that leads to a completed product and make it harder for the researcher to maintain the stance of the expert who makes the final pronouncement. Many experiments have sought to harness these possibilities in the interests of a more inclusive research process with wider resonance among participants. It remains to be seen whether these experiments will have an impact on research processes more broadly and help to change our expectations of what good research might be. At present, conventional journal publishing seems to be hanging on, thanks to its being embedded within deeply rooted systems of quality control and reputation-building. It may be that, in the future, new forms of publishing and research engagement will take hold, accompanied by new ways of building a reputation and assuring the quality of outputs.

A final significant set of challenges focus on the changing nature of the social reality that we inhabit and seek to understand. As online and offline modes of interaction become more integrated with one another and more seamlessly part of everyday experience, and as the Internet becomes blended into geographically and temporally located experiences through mobile, personalized, always-on technologies, the challenges for qualitative research practice multiply. Finding a field to study and rendering it as a researchable situation become more and more challenging as people flit between media in a constant play between contexts. Our responses may need to include more mobile, geo-located, and real-time research, possibly conducted using mobile devices ourselves, and we may have to accept the partiality of understanding that comes from being in lots of places at once, practicing different kinds of presence. We may find ourselves needing to relax the traditional reliance on sustained co-presence with the research setting, in cases in which it becomes harder to identify a sustained research setting to be in, and instead develop more fleeting research interactions, organized around a focus but spread out over time and space.

Along with these challenges of an everyday life that is multiply mediated and multiply contextual come difficulties in making substantiated claims about what it takes to understand any given situation. Our interventions may increasingly need to go against the flow of rapid and multiply mediated interactions, as we ask people to slow down, pause, and reflect on their circumstances. Efforts will need to be made to contextualize our research, possibly meaning that we need to take more efforts to see that our research is read and received appropriately. Either we simply put our thoughts out into the world and leave them to make their way, or we try to see the communication of research results as itself a form of engagement that involves building relationships. These engaged interventions (including what Marcus [1998] calls "circumstantial activism") would allow us to go with the flow of an increasingly mediated, mobile, and fragmented world, but develop a form of knowledge that is more than a fragmented "drive-by" social research. A social research embracing the contemporary and future Internet can still be based on careful commitments to developing a robust knowledge of something, for someone.

As the Internet develops, it is quite possible that qualitative research practice, and academic writing in general, will continue to develop new forms and push against the boundaries of what academic writing has previously been. As these developments take place, it will be more important than ever to reflect carefully on our writing practices and our quality criteria, taking care that we say exactly what it is that we feel entitled to say through our research experiences. By doing this, it will be possible to continue to produce methodologically careful, accurately circumscribed, evocative, interesting, and insightful research, as the Internet becomes a mundane technology for qualitative research.

6

SUGGESTIONS FOR FURTHER READING

THIS SELECTION of texts is necessarily a personal choice. I have recommended some general texts on qualitative research that I have found particularly helpful or pertinent to Internet research. On Internet culture, I have suggested some of the foundational readings that mapped out claims for the Internet as an appropriate field in which to study social interaction and complex social formations. I have also included some more recent texts that review the state of our personal relationships mediated through online and mobile interactions, and also texts that look at the current state of academic scholarship in the face of online developments. A list of texts giving methodological advice for online research then follows. I have then listed a necessarily arbitrary set of examples of qualitative and mixed-method Internet research, choosing texts that cover a wide range of different approaches and focusing on those that I think explain particularly well the approach that they take and give the reader the chance to explore its consequences. Finally, I identify some online resources that may be of interest in developing qualitative Internet research skills.

Qualitative Research and Writing

Coffey, A., & Atkinson, P. (1996). *Making sense of qualitative data: Complementary research strategies*. Thousand Oaks, CA: Sage Publications.
This book predates the widespread use of the Internet in qualitative research and thus does not address many of the specific issues that qualitative Internet researchers may face. It does, however, offer a very useful overview of different approaches to analysis of qualitative data, illustrating the diversity by applying these frameworks in turn to a single dataset.

Darlington, Y., & Scott, D. (2002). *Qualitative research in practice: Stories from the field*. Crows Nest, NSW: Allen and Unwin.
This book surveys researchers' real experiences of qualitative research projects, including research undertaken in contexts of practice such as social work, education, healthcare, and community work. The Internet is not directly addressed. This book does, however, provide an introduction to the experience of doing research and to the contingencies and decisions that may be faced along the way, which is applicable to many qualitative researchers, whether working online or offline.

Denzin, N. K. (1997). *Interpretive ethnography: Ethnographic practices for the 21st century*. Thousand Oaks, CA: Sage Publications.
This text explores ethnography as a form of intervention and specifically explores the implications of ethnographies as diverse ways of "writing culture." Denzin considers various forms of experimental ethnographic texts and explores the potential for transformation of the standard ethnographic narrative. Although the Internet features only in passing, it is possible to see some of the experiments in digital ethnography discussed in Chapter 4 of this volume as continuous with the spirit of attention to ethnographic form that Denzin describes.

Dicks, B., Mason, B., Coffey, A., & Atkinson, P. (2005). *Qualitative research and hypermedia: Ethnography for the digital age*. London: Sage.
This book acknowledges the pervasive influence of digital technologies in contemporary societies and explores ways in which they might be embraced within ethnographic work. The authors focus particularly on multimedia and hypermedia as means to present ethnographic work and hence do not focus specifically on online fieldwork. Rather, they look at ways in which diverse forms of media can be incorporated into both fieldwork and end product.

Glaser, B. G., & Strauss, A. L. (1967). *The discovery of grounded theory: Strategies for qualitative research*. Chicago: AldineTransaction.
This classic text sets out a highly influential model for qualitative analysis, stressing the need for the researcher to pay close and detailed attention to what the body of data itself has to say. This approach to theorizing grounded in the data is heavily cited as an ideal, although the precise steps to analysis laid out by Glaser and Strauss are rarely followed in their entirety.

Goodall, H. L. (2008). *Writing qualitative inquiry: Self, stories, and academic life*. Walnut Creek, CA: Left Coast Press.
Goodall explores a form of qualitative writing that gives a prominent place to the researcher's thoughts and experiences, and blends aspects of creative

writing into the account. He focuses particularly on what makes qualitative writing interesting and enjoyable to read, and offers advice aimed at making such writing more engaging for readers. Advice on the publishing process for qualitative writers is also included.

Hammersley, M., & Atkinson, P. (2007). *Ethnography: Principles in practice* (3rd ed.). London: Routledge.
This comprehensive overview of ethnographic methods offers sensible and theoretically informed advice for all stages of the ethnographic research process. The authors encourage a reflexive approach to ethnography, seeing the researcher as inherently part of the social world that he or she examines. They include some discussion of virtual ethnography and discuss some advantages to and drawbacks of the incorporation of online interactions within ethnographic approaches.

Marcus, G. (1995). Ethnography in/of the world system: The emergence of multi-sited ethnography. *Annual Review of Anthropology, 24*: 95–117.
This oft-cited text offers an overview of approaches to ethnographic field-work that move away from a single bounded fieldsite and explore other forms of focus, including following of objects, people, and narratives across sites. Although many of these approaches had previously been deployed by ethnographers to good effect, Marcus made a substantial contribution by naming and validating multisitedness as an ethnographic strategy.

Maxwell, J. A. (2005). *Qualitative research design: An interactive approach.* Thousand Oaks, CA: Sage.
This book identifies a systematic approach to the design of qualitative research projects, with extensive use of examples and exercises to carry out in order to help new researchers apply the advice to their own circumstances. The book also contains an example of a research proposal for a qualitative research project.

Silverman, D. (2006). *Interpreting qualitative data: Methods for analysing talk, text and interaction* (3rd ed.). London: Sage.
This text begins with an overview of qualitative research and looks at what is distinctive in the questions that it enables us to answer. Silverman then moves on to consider the analysis of different forms of data, looking at ethnography, interviews, texts, naturally occurring talk, and visual data. This includes a brief discussion of data collected via the Internet, such as e-mail interviews.

Silverman, D. (2009). *Doing qualitative research* (3rd ed.). London: Sage.
This introductory text gives a very helpful overview of the whole qualitative research process, including design, data collection, and analysis.

Tashakkori, A. (2006). *Mixed methodology: Combining qualitative and quantitative approaches.* Thousand Oaks, CA: Sage.
This book gives a balanced overview of the design and conduct of studies that combine qualitative and quantitative research approaches in various ways. A distinction is identified between mixed-method studies, which deploy different forms of data collection, and mixed-model studies, which involve a more systematic integration of qualitative and quantitative approaches throughout

the course of a study. Although the Internet does not specifically feature, there are some provocative ideas for a researcher interested in developing a combination of qualitative and quantitative approaches to Internet-derived data.

van Maanen, J. (1988). *Tales of the field: On writing ethnography*. Chicago: University of Chicago Press.

Van Maanen focuses on the different styles of writing prevalent in ethnographic research, discussing examples of both matter-of-fact realist ethnographic writing and more experimental and confessional styles. Reading this book is very useful at any stage of a qualitative writing project, to encourage reflection on the textual devices we can use to bring the field alive for readers.

Internet Culture

Bakardjieva, M. (2005). *Internet society: the Internet in everyday life*. London: Sage.

This book focuses on everyday experiences of the Internet, looking at the adoption processes and contextualization of the Internet into people's specific circumstances. Much of the research is based on conventional face-to-face techniques, interviewing people in the home about their Internet usage. There is, however, some important material here for those who use the medium of the Internet for their research interactions, in the attention that Bakardjieva gives to the "little behaviour genres" that help people to creatively appropriate the Internet and make sense of it within everyday life. Qualitative Internet researchers do well to remember that the Internet probably means quite different things to their research participants and can be experienced in diverse ways.

Baym, N. K. (2010). *Personal connections in the digital age*. Cambridge: Polity.

This book offers a thorough review of the potential consequences of the Internet for the conduct of personal relationships. Baym rejects a technologically determinist notion that the Internet might straightforwardly have effects on our relationships and focuses on the emergent qualities of diverse forms of Internet communication in various circumstances. The book explores both group contexts and dyadic interactions, taking place in a variety of different forms of Internet and mobile media. Baym is particularly conscious of the extent to which mobile devices are both themselves implicated in new ways of forging relationships and offer new ways in which to experience the Internet and incorporate it into our lives.

Borgman, C. L. (2007). *Scholarship in the digital age: Information, infrastructure, and the Internet*. Cambridge, MA: MIT Press.

This book reviews the impacts of the Internet on scholarship, looking for both changes and continuities in the way that academic research is carried out and disseminated. Borgman examines the responses to the massive increase in data availability that some disciplines have experienced, and explores the challenges and opportunities for our communications infrastructures. This book describes changes that have occurred, explores the policy context that frames the opportunities and risks that academic researchers adapting to the Internet face, and looks to the future of a scholarly research publishing system ever more embedded in a digital world.

Castells, M. (2002). *The Internet galaxy: Reflections on the Internet, business, and society*. Oxford: Oxford University Press.
This broad-ranging book examines the advent and growth of the Internet in the context of Castell's formulation of the network society, exploring cultural, political, and commercial aspects of contemporary social formations as enabled by the Internet.

Dutton, W. H., & Jeffreys, P. W. (Eds.). (2010). *World wide research: Reshaping the sciences and humanities*. Cambridge, MA: MIT Press.
This edited book explores the advent of e-science and e-research in a wide variety of contexts, looking both at the new forms of research that have been enabled and the various disciplinary contexts and policy pressures that shape these developments.

Jones, S. G. (Ed.). (1997). *Virtual culture*. London, Sage.
This early collection of papers on the culture of the Internet contained some significant contributions on the study of online communities and the contextualization of Internet activities as meaningful social activity. This was highly influential at a time when the status of the Internet as a site for rich and meaningful social interactions was still held in some doubt in public discourse. Steve Jones' introductory chapter carefully analyzes the role of the Internet in contemporary life and examines the debate around the role of the Internet as community.

Jones, S. G. (Ed.). (1998). *Cybersociety 2.0: Revisiting computer-mediated communication and community*. Newbury Park, CA: Sage.
This reworking of the collection *Cybersociety,* published in 1995, contains some influential chapters that stake a claim for the Internet as a site of meaningful social interactions, amenable to exploration by using adaptations of recognizable social research methodologies. In particular, Nancy Baym's chapter on the emergence of online community was one of the most influential in shaping an understanding of what online communities might be and how they should be studied. Steve Jones explores various notions of community as applied to the Internet and notes the spatial biases inherent in some operationalizations of community.

Rheingold, H. (1993). *The virtual community: Homesteading on the electronic frontier* Reading, MA: Addison-Wesley.
This book is a semi-popular account of the WELL, a California-based bulletin board system. Howard Rheingold writes as a journalist rather than a social scientist. Nonetheless, his evocative descriptions of online interactions and the role that they play in his everyday family life are useful for qualitative Internet researchers wanting to find ways to write about the Internet that will bring it to life as a form of recognizable everyday social interaction and yet still draw out what is special, distinctive, and surprising about it.

Methods Texts Focusing on the Internet

Buchanan, E. A. (2004). *Readings in virtual research ethics: Issues and controversies*. Hershey, PA: Information Science.
This edited collection offers a range of positions on ethical conduct in online research, discussing the official recommendations of the Association of Internet Researchers Ethics Working Committee (see below), together with chapters exploring ethical research conduct as negotiated for a variety of different methodologies and a range of challenging and sensitive online research environments.

Ess, C., & AoIR Ethics Working Committee. (2002). Ethical decision-making and Internet research: recommendations from the AoIR ethics working committee. Retrieved from http://www.aoir.org/reports/ethics.pdf
This report outlines the recommendations adopted by the Association of Internet Researchers for ethical research conduct among members carrying out research on the Internet. The report accepts that research circumstances and analytic approaches vary widely, and hence there is no stable answer to whether or not, for example, informed consent is required for specific kinds of online setting. Instead the report offers a series of questions that the researcher should ask him- or herself in order to arrive at a stance on ethical conduct in a particular research situation.

Garcia, A. C., Standlee, A. I., Bechkoff, J., & Cui, Y. (2009). Ethnographic approaches to the Internet and computer-mediated communication. *Journal of Contemporary Ethnography, 38*(1): 52–84.
This review offers a very useful summary of the practical and analytic challenges that online ethnographers face. The authors describe a series of adjustments that ethnographers may need to make to conventional practices in order to adapt to the demands of online settings. These adjustments include changes in the definition of fieldsites, the formation and maintenance of relations with participants, and the assurance of ethical research conduct.

Garton, L., Haythornthwaite, C., & Wellman, B. (1997). Studying online social networks. *Journal of Computer Mediated Communication, 3*(1). Retrieved from http://jcmc.indiana.edu/vol3/issue1/garton.html
This article very clearly lays out the background of social network analysis and discusses various ways in which it applies to the Internet as it was at the time of writing. Many aspects of the Internet have, of course, changed since the paper was written, but it remains a useful introduction to the concepts of social network analysis that Internet researchers might deploy.

Hine, C. (2000). *Virtual ethnography*. London: Sage.
This book explores the application of ethnographic principles to the study of the Internet, arguing that it is a mistake to treat the "virtual" as if it were a single phenomenon inherently apart from real life. Instead, we should treat the Internet as both culture and cultural artifact, since it operates both as a conduit of everyday life and as a technology variously constructed by users with quite different interpretations of what it means for them. It is suggested that the Internet ethnographer can usefully draw on his or her own online interactions to add an

experiential depth to his or her descriptions of what he or she finds online. The book explores a case study of a media event, exploring the ways in which users and mass media attribute meaning to the Internet. It combines e-mail interviews with website developers and discussion group participants together with analysis of websites, discussion forum postings, and mass media coverage.

Hine, C. (Ed.). (2005). *Virtual methods: Issues in social research on the Internet.* Oxford: Berg.
This collection gathers together both qualitative and quantitative research perspectives using case studies to examine some common methodological concerns raised by the Internet. Contributions are grouped into two sections, one on "research relationships and online relationships" and one on "research sites and strategies." The introductory chapter discusses the advent of the Internet as a source of both innovation and anxiety in research methods, as questions arise about the extent to which established methods and principles continue to be relevant to virtual interactions.

James, N., & Busher, H. (2009). *Online interviewing.* London: Sage.
This book focuses on strategies for successful online interviewing. Drawing on references to a wide range of sociological work focused on the Internet and beyond, the authors argue that online interviewing is more than a technique to be learned. Instead, successful strategies have to be designed by researchers in context. James and Busher explore some of the epistemological, practical, and ethical dilemmas that can arise along the way, drawing heavily on their own research experiences in academic and educational workplaces. This book would be particularly useful for researchers who already have a good grasp of the principles of interviewing as a methodology and the nature of interview data.

Johns, M. D., Chen, S.-L. S., & Hall, G. J. (Eds.). (2004). *Online social research: Methods, issues, & ethics.* New York, Peter Lang.
This edited collection contains discussion by some experienced Internet researchers of ethical issues faced by a variety of research methods and approaches that may be deployed on the Internet, including interviews, focus groups, observation, and surveys. The authors also discuss the process of gaining approval from Institutional Review Boards or ethics committees.

Jones, S. (Ed.). (1999). *Doing Internet research: Critical issues and methods for examining the net.* Thousand Oaks, CA: Sage.
This early text on Internet research methods gathers together some groundbreaking work exploring the extent to which existing methods apply to online interactions. Chapters cover both qualitative and quantitative perspectives, including discursive and rhetorical analysis, surveys, website analysis, social network analysis, and online ethnography. The preface argues for a recognition that Internet research is always, in some sense, social research, and suggests that the Internet should be seen as grounded in and part of offline social life.

Mann, C., & Stewart, F. (2000). *Internet communication and qualitative research: A handbook for researching online.* London: Sage.
This textbook gives advice on a range of different research approaches using the Internet, including online ethnography, e-mail interviews, and online

focus groups. It draws particularly on the experience of the authors in conducting research with students and schoolchildren using these methods. Although technologies have moved on significantly since the book was written, much of its practical advice about the design of projects for which online methods are appropriate and its discussion of the ethics and practice of online research remain highly relevant. Particularly pertinent is the question of how far online methods can be used to study real-life research problems, balancing out the constraints and opportunities of online research.

Markham, A. N., & Baym, N.K. (Eds.). (2008). *Internet inquiry: Conversations about method*. Thousand Oaks, CA: Sage.

This book gathers together several Internet researchers to discuss how they made methodological decisions in their work. Contributions are organized as conversations between contributors on the following topics: defining the boundaries of a project; combining online and offline research; attending to privacy; addressing gender and sexuality; producing work that is meaningful across time, space, and cultures, given the shifting and contextual nature of the Internet; and defining quality in qualitative Internet research. The focus throughout is on exploring how sensible, defensible methodological decisions can be made according to the very specific and shifting circumstances that a qualitative Internet researcher will encounter.

McKee, H. A., & Porter, J. E. (2009). *The ethics of Internet research: A rhetorical, case-based process*. New York: Peter Lang.

This book explores ethical issues that may be faced in an Internet approach, drawing on interviews with researchers themselves. A case-based presentation identifies problems that may be encountered and potential ethical responses across the research project life-cycle.

Miller, D., & Slater, D. (2000). *The Internet: An ethnographic approach*. Oxford: Berg.

The methodological premise of this book is that researchers of the Internet should not begin online, nor even necessarily assume that there is such a thing as "the virtual." Instead, the ethnographic strategy deployed here is to identify a group of people (in this case, Trinidadians both living at home and abroad) and find out what the Internet means to them. Where the researchers do venture online, it is into online spaces identified as significant to the research participants and with an aim to contextualize online activities within the offline spaces within which they are made relevant.

Paccagnella, L. (1997). Getting the seats of your pants dirty: Strategies for ethnographic research on virtual communities. *Journal of Computer-Mediated Communication 3*(1). Retrieved from http://jcmc.indiana.edu/vol3/issue1/paccagnella.html

This frequently cited paper was one of the first comprehensive discussions of the extent to which existing principles of ethnographic research applied to the Internet. Paccagnella argues for an immersive approach to study of the Internet, utilizing the existing ethnographic principle of learning by doing. He argues for some caution in accepting the accounts given by online informants at face value and discusses the dilemmas posed by the opportunities for covert research that the Internet affords. He also explores the extent to which automated collection and systematic analysis of Internet data could augment the online ethnographer's toolkit.

Schneider, S. M., & Foot, K. A. (2004). The web as an object of study. *New Media & Society, 6*(1): 114–122.

The authors divide studies of the web into three main families of approach: the discursive or rhetorical approach, which focuses on the textual or visual content of a website; structural analysis, which looks either at the features of an individual website or applies techniques such as network analysis to emergent structures across websites; and sociocultural analysis, which often deploys ethnographic methods to explore the web as it becomes meaningful to producers and users. The authors propose their own web sphere analysis as a combination of these approaches.

Seale, C., Charteris-Black, J., MacFarlane, A., & McPherson, A. (2010). Interviews and Internet forums: A comparison of two sources of qualitative data. *Qualitative Health Research, 20*(5): 595–606.

This article explores the possibilities of using observations of online discussion groups to complement or replace conventional interviews in health research. A systematic comparison of these different sources of data is presented. Although interviews have the advantage in terms of focused discussion of the topic, the ability to probe for contextual details, and a much more straightforward management of ethical issues, online observations gain in the frankness of discussions that can be observed.

Thelwall, M. (2009). *Introduction to Webometrics: Quantitative web research for the social sciences.* San Rafael, CA: Morgan and Claypool.

This text may be somewhat of a surprise in a list aimed at providing resources for qualitative researchers, but as I have argued, the sheer amount of data available on the Internet can encourage a qualitative researcher to draw on quantitative techniques at some point. Thelwall has conducted many inventive studies exploring the use of "found data" from the Internet, and he draws on these experiences here to discuss practical techniques that other researchers may wish to use.

Wilson, S. M., & Peterson, L. C. (2002). The anthropology of online communities. *Annual Review of Anthropology, 31*(1): 449–467.

This review provides a comprehensive overview of anthropological approaches to the Internet. It particularly makes the point that the Internet itself is a cultural product and, as such, thoroughly amenable to anthropological enquiry. The review focuses on literature relating to online community, identity and questions of power, ideology, and the digital divide. The pace of technological change is a potential challenge for anthropologists and has promoted some unwarranted speculation on radical social and cultural consequences of the Internet. Thus far, Wilson and Peterson argue, no radical transformation of anthropology itself has been required, and existing anthropological dispositions have proved adequate for exploring the evolving Internet.

Examples of Qualitative and Mixed-Method Internet Research

Baym, N. K. (2000). *Tune in, log on: Soaps, fandom and online community.* Thousand Oaks, CA: Sage.

This ethnographic study of an online soap opera discussion group was one of the early studies rigorously to apply the notion of ethnography to online interactions. Baym suggests that the group counts as a community in three respects: as an online community, as an audience, and as a community of practice. She draws on a combination of her own participation in the group, in-depth analysis of a selection of messages, and various interviews and surveys among participants. The upshot is a thorough and well-rounded discussion of the norms and values of the group, focusing on the shared practices, humor, and sense of social hierarchy that pervade the group.

Boellstorff, T. (2008). *Coming of age in Second Life: an anthropologist explores the virtually human.* Princeton, NJ: Princeton University Press.

This book describes an ethnographic project conducted in Second Life, the graphical virtual world in which users are represented by avatars and can move around, buy and sell artifacts and real estate, and communicate by means of public and private text and audio channels. Boellstorff argues for the application of classical ethnographic principles to wholly online settings. His writing deploys a careful description of the details of embodiment and interaction in Second Life with many images taken from his experiences and evocative examples of interactions from the perspectives of different users. He argues that, although the fieldsite may, in this instance, be based wholly online, it is still legitimately a place to study the conditions of contemporary existence. According to contemporary anthropological thinking, all fieldsites are in some sense arbitrarily bounded, and, in this, he argues, the choice of Second Life as a fieldsite is no different to other choices the anthropologist might make about how to define a site to study.

boyd, d. m. (2008). Taken out of context: American teen sociality in networked publics. Doctoral thesis submitted to Graduate Division, University of California, Berkeley. Retrieved from http://www.danah.org/papers/TakenOutOfContext.pdf

This Ph.D. thesis explored the use of social networking sites by American teenagers. A combination of face-to-face and online interviews, online observation, and unstructured offline observations of teenagers hanging out was used to explore how teenagers made use of social networking sites and how this activity made sense within their lives more broadly. The framework of "networked publics" is used to understand the sense of place and imagined audience conceived through use of social networking sites.

Bury, R. (2005). *Cyberspaces of their own: Female fandoms online.* New York: Peter Lang.

This study of online fandom uses a combination of survey, e-mail interview, and observation to conduct an ethnographic exploration of online community and its relationship with the objects of fandom. The writing brings together a wide range of theoretical concepts from media and cultural studies and Internet research with a particular focus on gender, spatiality, and embodiment, and brings to life the experience of participants through extensive use of quotations from interviews and messages sent to the dedicated research list that Bury set up.

Constable, N. (2003). *Romance on a global stage: Pen pals, virtual ethnography and "mail order" marriages.* Berkeley: University of California Press.
Constable studied websites and online discussion forums used by prospective partners in transnational marriages, particularly focusing on men in the United States and prospective partners in China, Russia, and the Philippines. Constable conducts a multisited study that combines online interviews and observation of online interactions with face-to-face interviews with the various parties to the interactions.

Davis, M., Bolding, G., Hart, G., Sherr, L., & Elford, J. (2004). Reflecting on the experience of interviewing online: Perspectives from the Internet and HIV study in London. *AIDS Care, 16*(8): 944–952.
This paper describes a study that used both face-to-face interviews and online synchronous interviews in chat rooms to explore gay men's sexual practices. The comparison suggests that, although the chat room interviews were sometimes popular with interviewees, they did have drawbacks as a data collection method. Online interviews took longer and produced less words than face-to-face interviews. The interviewer found himself adopting a quite distinctive text-speak style in interviews, very different from the face-to-face discussions, and the flow of conversation was often broken up because of the lack of immediate visual feedback.

Dirksen, V., Huizing, A., & Smit, B. (2010). Piling on layers of understanding: The use of connective ethnography for the study of (online) work practices. *New Media & Society, 12*(7): 1045–1063.
This study deployed analysis of log files as an adjunct to ethnographic work. A combination of online and offline research methods is used, in particular informed by social network analysis of log files of online interactions within a complex organization to augment members' accounts of their practices and connections.

Efimova, L. A. (2009). Passion at work: Blogging practices of knowledge workers. Novay PhD Research Series, Vol. 24. Enschede: Novay. Retrieved from http://igitur-archive.library.uu.nl/dissertations/2009-0626-200434/UUindex.html
Efomiva conducted a highly reflexive study of blogging practices, as a blogger herself both before and during the study. Her work incorporates participant observation, interviews, analysis of blog content, and analysis of emergent structures, through systematic analysis of commenting, linking, and tagging practices.

Erickson, I. (2010). Geography and community: New forms of interaction among people and places. *American Behavioral Scientist, 53*(8): 1194–1207.
Erickson's paper explores usage of two micro-blogging tools, Twitter and Jaiku, in terms of the role of location in their sense of community. The argument is

based on in-depth face-to-face interviews with users combined with analysis of their micro-blogging activity. The paper makes an argument that the contrasting design of Jaiku and Twitter leads to very different outcomes in terms of spatiality and community. To make this paper comprehensible for an audience who may not have used micro-blogging, and to make it accessible as an argument about community and spatiality in contemporary life more generally, Erickson makes a very careful explanation of the forms of interaction that Twitter and Jaiku afford and the ways in which they differ.

Foot, K. A., & Schneider, S. M. (2006). *Web campaigning.* Cambridge, MA: MIT Press.
This book offers a significant example of a large-scale corpus-based study of online phenomena. Foot and Schneider write about the use of the Internet in the U.S. electoral campaigns of 2000, 2002, and 2004. They collected campaign websites produced during these elections and conducted a systematic analysis of the various features, in terms of campaign organization and relationship with the electorate, that they displayed.

Herring, S. C., Kouper, I., Paolillo, J. C., Scheidt, L. A., Tyworth, M., Welsch, P., Wright, E., & Yu, N. (2005). *Conversations in the blogosphere: An analysis "from the bottom up."* Proceedings of the 38th Annual HI International Conference on System Sciences. Big Island, Hawaii, USA, IEEE.
This multimethods study combines qualitative and quantitative approaches to investigate the extent to which blogging should be seen as a "conversational" practice. The quantitative study uses social network analysis of blog interlinkages and visualizes the patterns of linkage between blogs, in order to investigate the varying density of connections between blogs. Many blogs turn out to have few links to others, but some intensely connected groups of blogs do emerge. The qualitative study focused on the extent to which authors refer to one another's blogs in the content of their posts and comments, focusing on pairs of reciprocally linked blogs identified in the social network analysis. Quantitative and qualitative research converge on the insight that, although the blogosphere is conversational in parts, the majority of blogs are much more isolated and do not participate in sustained links or mutual commentary with other blogs.

Kendall, L. (2002). *Hanging out in the virtual pub: Masculinities and relationships online.* Berkeley: University of California Press.
This early ethnographic study of a MUD (multiuser dungeon—a text-based, real-time online space) is notable for its use of scene-setting vignettes that are used to bring the interactions to life for the reader and to emphasize the everyday nature of the interactions in which Kendall participated. The metaphor of the pub is used to capture the public, informal, yet socially patterned and highly masculinized form of interaction that took place in the forum. Kendall thus explores the extent to which norms of gendered behavior online are continuous with those prevailing offline. Kendall's work is based on 3 years of participation in the group, supplemented by informal online interviews, face-to-face interviews, and attendance at face-to-face meetings between participants.

Miller, D. (2011). *Tales from Facebook*. Cambridge: John Wiley & Sons.
Miller explores the role of Facebook in the diverse lives of Trinidadian users. His approach is ethnographic and founded in his long-term research interest in Trinidad. The writing is particularly notable for the care that Miller takes to protect the identities of his informants while also giving a rich picture of lives as lived with and through Facebook. He achieves this by presenting vignettes that, while apparently the stories of individuals, are in fact composites true to the spirit of what he was told but not based on any single person.

Nardi, B. A. (2010). *My life as a night elf priest: An anthropological account of World of Warcraft*. Ann Arbor: University of Michigan Press.
Nardi reports on an ethnographic study of the massively multiplayer online game World of Warcraft. The ethnography involved her playing the game extensively and reporting on her own experiences and observation and interviews with other participants. She analyzes her experiences through a theoretical frame of play as aesthetic experience. The book offers a useful example of an immersive ethnographic study based largely on online experiences, analyzed through an analytic frame with a wider significance beyond the Internet.

Orgad, S. S. (2005b). *Storytelling online: Talking breast cancer on the Internet*. New York: Peter Lang.
Orgad studied women who had used the Internet to discuss their experiences of breast cancer, making use of both online and offline interviews to allow these women to tell her about their experiences. She explores the ways in which telling their stories online on websites and in discussion forums becomes a significant part of these women's experience and looks at factors that structure their storytelling. The analytic frame of "storytelling" enables Orgad to pay careful analytic attention both to the stories that she finds online and the stories that are constructed in the online and offline interview settings.

Wen, K.-Y., McTavish, F., Kreps, G., Wise, M., & Gustafson, D. (2011). From diagnosis to death: A case study of coping with breast cancer as seen through online discussion group messages. *Journal of Computer-Mediated Communication, 16*(2): 331–361.
Qualitative content analysis based on a grounded theory approach is used in this study to explore the patterns of discussion in an online support group for cancer patients. The study is distinctive in its focus on one patient's involvement in the group, tracing her experiences of the group in relation to the progression of the disease. This approach allows the authors to explore how the uses made of the group might vary in context of the changing disease experiences of patients. It is methodologically innovative both in its attention to temporal aspects of the discussion group and in linking patterns of online discussion to wider contexts.

Online Resources for Qualitative Internet Research

There is, of course, no clear dividing line between online resources and the texts described above, since most of these texts can be found online in one form or another, and many resources that begin online still migrate into conventional publications eventually. Here, however, are a few resources that are primarily designed to be used online and that offer something particularly helpful for qualitative researchers who plan to venture into online fieldwork. I have deliberately avoided including software tools since these can date so quickly and can be so specific to a particular project. I also avoided recommending blogs, since researchers can be quite inconsistent in maintaining them, and even the best research blogs can often be quite ephemeral. Instead, I have focused on broader training and survey resources that I hope will have more longevity and a wider applicability.

Association of Internet Researchers

http://aoir.org/
A membership organization that brings together researchers across disciplines around an interest in researching online phenomena. The organization maintains a wiki and a very useful mailing list, the archives of which will contain answers to many questions a qualitative Internet researcher might wish to ask.

Exploring Online Research Methods

http://www.restore.ac.uk/orm/learnerresources/resources.htm
This site reviews literature on online research methods and offers self-paced learning modules in use of online interviews and questionnaires, and in considering the ethics of online research.

Internet World Statistics

http://www.internetworldstats.com/
This commercially owned site collates statistics on Internet penetration and use across the world, including assessments of the prevalence of different languages, the penetration of broadband, and the uptake of Facebook. These statistics can be particularly useful when planning an international study, in order to assess how the conditions of Internet access and use may vary between countries.

Methods for Analysis of Media Content

http://www.restore.ac.uk/lboro/index.php
This resource compares approaches used in analyzing various forms of media content and offers links to literature and other resources on approaches,

including content analysis, frame analysis, and discourse analysis. It also presents a comparison of software to support media analysis.

Oxford Internet Institute

http://www.oii.ox.ac.uk/
This site offers access to a variety of publications on Internet policy, governance, and culture, including the Oxford Internet Surveys conducted every 2 years since 2003 on a representative sample of the U.K. population.

Pew Research Center's Pew Internet and American Life Project

http://www.pewinternet.org/
This site collects together a series of reports and surveys conducted since 1999, looking at who in the United States was using the Internet and what they were doing with it. The site offers both digested reports on specific topics and access to raw survey data.

Realities, Part of the ESRC National Centre for Research Methods

http://www.socialsciences.manchester.ac.uk/realities/
This website collects together a variety of resources, including reviews of innovative methods and links to presentations on a variety of qualitative research methods, including blog analysis, e-mail interviewing, visual methods, and music elicitation.

REFERENCES

Amit, V., Ed. (1999). *Constructing the field*. London, Routledge.

Anandarajan, M., & Anandarajan, A. (2010). *E-research collaboration: Theory, techniques and challenges*. Heidelberg: Springer.

Ashmore, M. (1989). *The reflexive thesis: Wrighting sociology of scientific knowledge*. Chicago: University of Chicago Press.

Atkinson, P. (1990). *The ethnographic imagination: Textual constructions of reality*. London: Routledge.

Atkinson, P., & Silverman, D. (1997). Kundera's Immortality: The interview society and the invention of the self. *Qualitative Inquiry, 3*(3), 304–325.

Bampton, R., & Cowton, C. (2002). The e-interview. *Forum Qualitative Sozialforschung/Forum: Qualitative Social Research, 3*(2). Retrieved from http://www.qualitative-research.net/index.php/fqs/article/viewArticle/848

Bassett, E. H., & O'Riordan, K. (2002). Ethics of Internet research: Contesting the human subjects research model. *Ethics and Information Technology, 4*(3), 233–247.

Baym, N. (1995). The emergence of community in computer-mediated communication. In S. Jones (Ed.), *Cybersociety* (pp. 138–163). Thousand Oaks, CA: Sage.

Baym, N. K. (2000). *Tune in, log on: Soaps, fandom and online community*. Thousand Oaks, CA: Sage.

Bazerman, C. (1981). What written knowledge does: Three examples of academic discourse. *Philosophy of the Social Sciences, 11*(3), 361–387.

Beaulieu, A. (2005). Sociable hyperlinks: An ethnographic approach to connectivity. In C. Hine (Ed.), *Virtual methods: Issues in social research on the Internet* (pp. 183–198). Oxford: Berg.

Beaulieu, A. (2010). Research Note. From co-location to co-presence: Shifts in the use of ethnography for the study of knowledge. *Social Studies of Science, 40*(3), 453–470.

Beaulieu, A., & Høybye, M. T. (2011). Studying mailing lists: Text, temporality, interaction and materiality at the intersection of e-mail and the web. In S. N. Hesse-Biber (Ed.), *The handbook of emergent technologies in social research* (pp. 257–274). New York: Oxford University Press.

Beaulieu, A., & Simakova, E. (2006). Textured connectivity: An ethnographic approach to understanding the timescape of hyperlinks. *Cybermetrics: International Journal of Scientometrics, Informetrics and Bibliometrics, 10.* Retrieved from http://www.cindoc.csic.es/cybermetrics/articles/v10i1p5.html

Beer, D., & Burrows, R. (2007). Sociology and, of and in Web 2.0: Some initial considerations. *Sociological Research Online, 12*(5). Retrieved from http://www.socresonline.org.uk/12/5/17.html

Boellstorff, T. (2008). *Coming of age in Second Life: An anthropologist explores the virtually human.* Princeton, NJ: Princeton University Press.

Boellstorff, T. (2010). A typology of ethnographic scales for virtual worlds. In W. S. Bainbridge (Ed.), *Online worlds: Convergence of the real and the virtual* (pp. 123–133). London: Springer.

Borgman, C. L. (2007). *Scholarship in the Digital Age: Information, infrastructure, and the Internet.* Cambridge, MA: MIT Press.

boyd, d. (2007). Why youth ♥ social network sites: The role of networked publics in teenage social life. In D. Buckingham (Ed.), *The John D. and Catherine T. MacArthur Foundation series on digital media and learning—youth, identity and digital media* (pp. 119–142). Cambridge, MA: MIT Press.

boyd, d. m. (2008). Taken out of context: American teen sociality in networked publics Doctoral thesis submitted to Graduate Division, University of California, Berkeley. Retrieved from http://www.danah.org/papers/TakenOutOfContext.pdf

Brettell, C. B. (1996). *When they read what we write: The politics of ethnography.* Westport, CT: Bergin & Garvey.

Bryman, A. (1984). The debate about quantitative and qualitative research: A question of method or epistemology? *British Journal of Sociology, 35*(1), 75–92.

Bryman, A., Becker, S., & Sempik, J. (2008). Quality criteria for quantitative, qualitative and mixed methods research: A view from social policy *International Journal of Social Research Methodology, 11*(4), 261–276.

Budka, P. (n.d.). MyKnet.org. K-Net Meeting Places. Retrieved May 7, 2011 from http://meeting.knet.ca/mp19/course/view.php?id=7

Bukvova, H., Kalb, H., & Schoop, E. (2010). *What we blog: A qualitative analysis of research blogs.* Publishing in the Networked World: Transforming the Nature of Communication, 14th International Conference on Electronic Publishing 16–18 June, 2010. Retrieved from http://dhanken.shh.fi/dspace/bitstream/10227/599/9/8bukvova_kalb_schoop.pdf

Burawoy, M. (2000). *Global ethnography: Forces, connections, and imaginations in a postmodern world.* Berkeley: University of California Press.

Burrell, J. (2009). The field site as a network: A strategy for locating ethnographic research. *Field Methods, 21*(2), 181–199.

Candea, M. (2007). Arbitrary locations: In defence of the bounded field-site. *Journal of the Royal Anthropological Institute, 13*(1), 167–184.

Cantó-Milà, N., & Seebach, S. (2011). Ana's friends. Friendship in online pro-ana communities. *Sociological Research Online, 16*(1). Retrieved from http://www.socresonline.org.uk/16/1/1.html

Carusi, A., & Reimer, T. (2010). Virtual research environment collaborative landscape study. Retrieved May 7, 2011, from http://www.jisc.ac.uk/media/documents/publications/vrelandscapereport.pdf.

Castells, M. (2002). *The Internet galaxy: Reflections on the Internet, business, and society*. Oxford: Oxford University Press.

Chou, S. W.-Y., Hunt, Y., Folkers, A., & Augustson, E. (2011). Cancer survivorship in the age of YouTube and social media: A narrative analysis. *Journal of Medical Internet Research, 13*(1), E7. Retrieved from http://www.jmir.org/2011/1/e7/

Clifford, J., & Marcus, G. E. (Eds.). (1986). *Writing culture: The poetics and politics of ethnography*. Berkeley: University of California Press.

Coffey, A. (1999). *The ethnographic self: Fieldwork and the representation of identity*. London: Sage.

Coffey, A., & Atkinson, P. (1996). *Making sense of qualitative data: Complementary research strategies*. Thousand Oaks, CA: Sage Publications.

Collins, H. M., & Yearley, S. (1992). Epistemological chicken. In A. Pickering (Ed.), *Science as practice and culture* (pp. 301–326). Chicago: University of Chicago Press.

Constable, N. (2003). *Romance on a global stage: Pen pals, virtual ethnography and "mail order" marriages*. Berkeley: University of California Press.

Cowan, J. (2008). Diary of a blog: Listening to kids in an elementary school library. *Teacher Librarian, 35*(5), 20–26.

Cummings, R. E., & Barton, M. (2008). *Wiki writing: Collaborative learning in the college classroom*. Ann Arbor: University of Michigan Press.

Dalsgaard, S. (2008). Facework on Facebook: The presentation of self in virtual life and its role in the US elections. *Anthropology Today, 24*(6), 8–12.

Darlington, Y., & Scott, D. (2002). *Qualitative research in practice: Stories from the field*. Crows Nest, NSW: Allen and Unwin.

Denzin, N. K. (1997). *Interpretive ethnography: Ethnographic practices for the 21st century*. Thousand Oaks, CA: Sage Publications.

Dicks, B., & Mason, B. (2011). Clickable data: Hypermedia and social research. In S. N. Hesse-Biber (Ed.), *The handbook of emergent technologies in social research* (pp. 133–157). New York: Oxford University Press.

Dicks, B., Mason, B., Coffey, A., & Atkinson, P. (2005). *Qualitative research and hypermedia: Ethnography for the digital age*. London: Sage.

Dicks, B., Soyinka, B., & Coffey, A. (2006). Multimodal ethnography. *Qualitative Research, 6*(1), 77–96.

Dirksen, V., Huizing, A., & Smit, B. (2010). Piling on layers of understanding: The use of connective ethnography for the study of (online) work practices. *New Media & Society, 12*(7), 1045–1063.

Dourish, P., Graham, C., Randall, D., & Rouncefield, M. (2010). Theme issue on social interaction and mundane technologies. *Personal and Ubiquitous Computing, 14*(3), 171–180.

Drotner, K. (2008). Leisure is hard work: Digital practices and future competencies. In D. Buckingham (Ed.), *John D. and Catherine T. MacArthur Foundation series on digital media and learning—Youth, identity and digital media* (pp. 167–184). Buckingham. Cambridge, MA: MIT Press.

Dutton, W. H., Helsper, E. J., & Gerber, M. M. (2010). The Internet in Britain 2009. Oxford: Oxford Internet Institute. Retrieved from http://www.oii.ox.ac.uk/research/oxis/OxIS2009_Report.pdf

Dutton, W. H., & Jeffreys, P. W. (Eds.). (2010). *World wide research: Reshaping the sciences and humanities*. Cambridge, MA: MIT Press.

Ebner, M., Mühlburger, H., Schaffert, S., Schiefner, M., Reinhardt, W., & Wheeler, S. (2010). Getting granular on Twitter: Tweets from a conference and their limited usefulness for non-participants. In N. Reynolds & M. Turcsányi-Szabó (Eds.), *Key competencies in the knowledge society. IFIP advances in information and communication technology* (vol. 324, pp. 102–113). Boston: Springer.

Efimova, L. A. (2009). Passion at work: Blogging practices of knowledge workers. Novay PhD Research Series, Vol. 24. Enschede: Novay. Retrieved from http://igitur-archive.library.uu.nl/dissertations/2009-0626-200434/UUindex.html

Ess, C., & AoIR Ethics Working Committee. (2002). Ethical decision-making and Internet research: Recommendations from the AoIR ethics working committee Retrieved from http://www.aoir.org/reports/ethics.pdf

Eysenbach, G., & Till, J. E. (2001). Ethical issues in qualitative research on internet communities. *British Medical Journal, 323*(7321), 1103–1105.

Fabian, J. (1983). *Time and the other: How anthropology makes its object*. New York: Columbia University Press.

Fabian, J. (1991). *Time and the work of anthropology: Critical essays, 1971–1991*. Amsterdam: Harwood Academic Publishers.

Falzon, M. A. (2009). *Multi-sited ethnography: Theory, praxis and locality in contemporary research*. Farnham: Ashgate.

Farnsworth, J., & Austrin, T. (2010). The ethnography of new media worlds? Following the case of global poker. *New Media & Society, 12*(7), 1120–1136.

Fielding, N., & Cisneros-Puebla, C. A. (2009). CAQDAS-GIS convergence toward a new integrated mixed method research practice? *Journal of Mixed Methods Research, 3*(4), 349–370.

Fitzgerald, R., & Findlay, J. (2011). Collaborative research tools: Using wikis and team learning systems to collectively create new knowledge. In S. N. Hesse-Biber (Ed.), *The handbook of emergent technologies in social research* (pp. 300–319). New York: Oxford University Press.

Flicker, S., Haans, D., & Skinner, H. (2004). Ethical dilemmas in research on Internet communities. *Qualitative Health Research, 14*(1), 124–134.

Foot, K. A., & Schneider, S. M. (2006). *Web campaigning*. Cambridge, MA: MIT Press.

Forte, M. C. (2004). Co-construction and field creation: Website development as both an instrument and relationship in action research. In E. Buchanan (Ed.),

Virtual research ethics: Issues and controversies (pp. 222–248). Hershey, PA: Idea Group.

Forte, M. C. (2005). Centering the links: Understanding cybernetic patterns of co-production, circulation and consumption. In C. Hine (Ed.), *Virtual methods: Issues in social research on the Internet* (pp. 93–106). Oxford: Berg.

Forte, M. C. (2006). Amerindian@Caribbean: Internet indigeneity in the electronic generation of Carib and Taino identities. In K. Landezlius (Ed.), *Native on the net: Indigenous and diasporic peoples in the virtual age* (pp. 132–151). London: Routledge.

Gaffney, D., Gilbert, S., & Pearce, I. (2011). 140kit: Regarding Twitter's API Rules and Data Export. Retrieved February 25, 2011, from http://140kit.com/documents/Regarding_API_Change.pdf.

Garcia, A. C., Standlee, A. I., Bechkoff, J., & Cui, Y. (2009). Ethnographic approaches to the Internet and computer-mediated communication. *Journal of Contemporary Ethnography, 38*(1), 52–84.

Garton, L., Haythornthwaite, C., & Wellman, B. (1997). Studying online social networks. *Journal of Computer Mediated Communication, 3*(1). Retrieved from http://jcmc.indiana.edu/vol3/issue1/garton.html

Glaser, B. G., & Strauss, A. L. (1967). *The discovery of grounded theory: Strategies for qualitative research.* Chicago: AldineTransaction.

Goldman, E. (2008). Search engine bias and the demise of search engine utopianism. In A. Spink & M. Zimmer (Eds.), *Web search* (pp. 121–133). Berlin: Springer.

Goodall, H. L. (2000). *Writing the new ethnography.* Walnut Creek, CA: Alta Mira.

Goodall, H. L. (2008). *Writing qualitative inquiry: Self, stories, and academic life.* Walnut Creek, CA: Left Coast Press.

Gray, N., Klein, J., Noyce, P., Sesselberg, T., & Cantrill, J. (2005). Health information-seeking behaviour in adolescence: The place of the internet. *Social Science & Medicine, 60*(7), 1467–1478.

Gregg, M. (2006). Feeling ordinary: Blogging as conversational scholarship. *Continuum: Journal of Media and Culture Studies, 20*(2), 147–160.

Guba, E. G., & Lincoln, Y. S. (1989). *Fourth generation evaluation.* Newbury Park, CA: Sage.

Guimarães, M. J. L. (2005). Doing anthropology in cyberspace: Fieldwork boundaries and social environments. In C. Hine (Ed.), *Virtual methods: Issues in social research on the Internet* (pp. 141–156). Oxford: Berg.

Gupta, A., & Feguson, J. (1997). *Anthropological locations: Boundaries and grounds of a field science.* Berkeley: University of California Press.

Halavais, A. (2006). Scholarly blogging: Moving toward the visible college. In A. Bruns and J. Jacobs (Eds.), *Uses of blogs* (pp. 117–126). New York: Peter Lang.

Hall, G. (2008). *Digitize this book!: The politics of new media, or why we need open access now.* Minneapolis: University of Minnesota Press.

Hannerz, U. (2003). Being there... and there... and there! Reflections on multisite ethnography. *Ethnography, 4*(2), 201–216.

Harvey, K. J., Brown, B., Crawford, P., Macfarlane, A., & McPherson, A. (2007). "Am I normal?" Teenagers, sexual health and the internet. *Social Science & Medicine, 65*(4), 771–781.

Hastrup, K. (1990). The ethnographic present: A reinvention. *Cultural Anthropology, 5*(1), 45–61.

Herring, S. (1996). Linguistic and critical analysis of computer-mediated communication: Some ethical and scholarly considerations. *The Information Society, 12*, 153–168.

Herring, S. C. (2010). Web content analysis: Expanding the paradigm. In J. Hunsinger, L. Klastrup & M. Allen (Eds.), *International handbook of internet research* (pp. 233–249). Netherlands: Springer.

Herring, S. C., Kouper, I., Paolillo, J. C., Scheidt, L. A., Tyworth, M., Welsch, P., Wright, E., & Yu, N. (2005). *Conversations in the blogosphere: An analysis "from the bottom up."* Proceedings of the 38th Annual HI International Conference on System Sciences Big Island, Hawaii, USA, IEEE

Herring, S. C., Scheidt, L. A., Kouper, I., & Wright, E. (2006). Longitudinal content analysis of weblogs: 2003–2004. In M. Tremayne (Ed.), *Blogging, citizenship, and the future of media* (pp. 3–20). London: Routledge.

Hey, T., & Trefethen, A. E. (2002). The UK e-Science core programme and the Grid. *Future Generation Computing Systems, 18*(8), 1017–1031.

Hine, C. (2000). *Virtual ethnography.* London: Sage.

Hine, C. (2005). Internet research and the sociology of cyber-social-scientific knowledge. *The Information Society, 21*(4), 239–248.

Hine, C. (2007). Connective ethnography for the exploration of e-science. *Journal of Computer Mediated Communication, 12*(2). Retrieved from http://jcmc.indiana.edu/vol12/issue2/hine.html

Hine, C. (2008a). How can qualitative internet researchers define the boundaries of their projects? In A. N. Markham and N. Baym (Eds.), *Internet inquiry: Conversations about method* (pp. 1–20). Thousand Oaks, CA: Sage.

Hine, C. (2008b). *Systematics as cyberscience: Computers, change and continuity in science.* Cambridge, MA: MIT Press.

Hine, C. (2011). Towards ethnography of television on the internet: A mobile strategy for exploring mundane interpretive activities. *Media Culture and Society, 33*(4), 581–596.

Hodkinson, P. (2008). Grounded theory and inductive research. In N. Gilbert (Ed.), *Researching social life* (3rd ed., pp. 80–100). London: Sage.

Hogan, B. (2008). Analyzing social networks via the Internet. In N. Fielding, R. M. Lee, & G. Blank (Eds.), *The Sage handbook of online research methods* (pp. 141–160). London: Sage.

Hookway, N. (2008). "Entering the blogosphere": Some strategies for using blogs in social research. *Qualitative Research, 8*(1), 91–113.

Howard, P. N. (2002). Network ethnography and the hypermedia organization: New media, new organizations, new methods. *New Media & Society, 4*(4), 550–574.

Hudson, J. M., & Bruckman, A. (2004). "Go away": Participant objections to being studied and the ethics of chatroom research. *Information Society, 20*(2), 127–139.

Illingworth, N. (2001). The Internet matters: Exploring the use of the internet as a research tool. *Sociological Research Online, 6*(2). Retrieved from http://www.socresonline.org.uk/6/2/illingworth.html

James, N., & Busher, H. (2006). Credibility, authenticity and voice: Dilemmas in online interviewing. *Qualitative Research, 6*(3), 403–420.

Johns, M. D., Chen, S.-L. S., & Hall, G. J. (Eds.). (2004). *Online social research: Methods, issues, & ethics.* New York: Peter Lang.

Jones, R. H. (2004). The problem of context in computer-mediated communication. In P. LeVine & R. Scollon (Eds.), *Discourse and technology: Multimodal discourse analysis.* (pp. 20–33). Washington, DC: Georgetown University Press.

Jones, S. G. (Ed.). (1995). *Cybersociety.* Newbury Park, CA: Sage.

Jones, S. G. (Ed.). (1997). *Virtual culture.* London: Sage.

Jones, S. G. (Ed.). (1998). *Cybersociety 2.0: Revisiting computer-mediated communication and community.* Newbury Park, CA: Sage.

Kazmer, M. M., & Xie, B. (2008). Qualitative interviewing in Internet studies: Playing with the media, playing with the method. *Information, Communication & Society, 11*(2), 257–278.

Kendall, L. (2002). *Hanging out in the virtual pub: Masculinities and relationships online.* Berkeley: University of California Press.

Kenny, A. J. (2005). Interaction in cyberspace: An online focus group. *Journal of Advanced Nursing, 49*(4), 414–422.

Kien, G. (2009). *Global technography: Ethnography in the age of mobility.* New York: Peter Lang.

Kivits, J. (2005). Online interviewing and the research relationship. In C. Hine (Ed.), *Virtual methods: Issues in social research on the Internet* (pp. 35–50). Oxford: Berg.

Knorr-Cetina, K. (1981). *The manufacture of knowledge: An essay on the constructivist and contextual nature of science.* Oxford: Pergamon.

Latour, B., & Woolgar, S. (1986). *Laboratory life: The construction of scientific facts* (2nd ed.). Princeton, NJ: Princeton University Press.

Law, J. (2004). *After method: Mess in social science research.* London: Routledge.

Leander, K. M., & McKim, K. K. (2003). Tracing the everyday "sitings" of adolescents on the Internet: A strategic adaptation of ethnography across online and offline spaces. *Education, Communication & Information, 3*(2), 211–240.

Lee, R. M. (2000). *Unobtrusive methods in social research.* Buckingham: Open University Press.

Lenhart, A., Purcell, K., Smith, A., & Zickuhr, K. (2010). Social media and mobile Internet use among teens and young adults. Washington, DC: Pew Internet and American Life Project, Pew Research Center. Retrieved from http://www.pewinternet.org/~/media//Files/Reports/2010/PIP_Social_Media_and_Young_Adults_Report_Final.pdf

Letierce, J., Passant, A., Breslin, J., & Decker, S. (2010a). *Understanding how Twitter is used to spread scientific messages.* WebSci10: Extending the Frontiers of Society On-Line, April 26–27th, 2010, Raleigh, North Carolina. Retrieved from US.http://journal.webscience.org/314/

Letierce, J., Passant, A., Breslin, J. G., & Decker, S. (2010b). *Using Twitter during an Academic Conference: The iswc2009 Use-Case.* Fourth International AAAI Conference on Weblogs and Social Media. Retrieved from http://www.aaai.org/ocs/index.php/ICWSM/ICWSM10/paper/view/1523

Levene, M. (2010). *An introduction to search engines and web navigation* (2nd ed.). Hoboken, NJ: Wiley.

Lewins, A., & Silver, C. (2007). *Using software in qualitative research: A step-by-step guide.* London: Sage.

Li, D., & Walejko, G. (2008). Splogs and abandoned blogs: The perils of sampling bloggers and their blogs. *Information, Communication & Society, 11*(2), 279–296.

Lincoln, Y. S., & Guba, E. (1985). *Naturalistic inquiry.* Beverley Hills, CA: Sage.

Lynch, M., & Woolgar, S. (Eds.). (1990). *Representation in scientific practice.* Cambridge, MA: MIT Press.

Lysloff, R. T. A. (2003). Musical community on the Internet: An on-line ethnography. *Cultural Anthropology, 18*(2), 233–263.

Madge, C., & O'Connor, H. (2002). Online with the e-mums: Exploring the internet as a medium for research. *Area, 34*(1), 92–102.

Malinowski, B. (1922/2003). *Argonauts of the Western Pacific: An account of native enterprise and adventure in the archipelagoes of Melanesian New Guinea.* London: Taylor and Francis.

Marcus, G. (1995). Ethnography in/of the world system: The emergence of multi-sited ethnography. *Annual Review of Anthropology, 24*, 95–117.

Marcus, G. (1998). *Ethnography through thick and thin.* Princeton, NJ: Princeton University Press.

Markham, A. N. (1998). *Life online: Researching real experience in virtual space.* Walnut Creek, CA: Altamira Press.

Markham, A. N. (2005). The methods, politics, and ethics of representation in online ethnography. In N. K. Denzin & Y. S. Lincoln (Eds.), *The Sage handbook of qualitative research* (3rd ed., pp. 793–820). Thousand Oaks, CA: Sage.

Markham, A. N. (2006). Ethic as method, method as ethic: A case for reflexivity in qualitative ICT research. *Journal of Information Ethics, 15*(2), 37–54.

Marshall, J. (2010). Ambiguity, oscillation and disorder: Online ethnography and the making of culture. *Cosmopolitan Civil Societies: An Interdisciplinary Journal 2*(3). Retrieved from http://epress.lib.uts.edu.au/ojs/index.php/mcs/article/view/1598/1859

Marwick, A. E., & boyd, d. (2011). I tweet honestly, I tweet passionately: Twitter users, context collapse, and the imagined audience. *New Media & Society, 13*(1), 114–133.

Mason, B., & Dicks, B. (2001). Going beyond the code. *Social Science Computer Review, 19*(4), 445–457.

Maxwell, J. A. (2010). Using numbers in qualitative research. *Qualitative Inquiry, 16*(6), 475–482.

Maynard, S., & O'Brien, A. (2010). Scholarly output: Print and digital—in teaching and research. *Journal of Documentation, 66*(3), 384–408.

McCoyd, J. L. M., & Kerson, T. S. (2006). Conducting intensive interviews using email. *Qualitative Social Work, 5*(3), 389–406.

Miller, D. (2011). *Tales from Facebook.* Cambridge: John Wiley & Sons.

Miller, D., & Slater, D. (2000). *The Internet: An ethnographic approach.* Oxford: Berg.

Morgan, D.L., & Lobe, B. (2011). Online focus groups. In S. N. Hesse-Biber (Ed.), *The handbook of emergent technologies in social research* (pp. 199–230). New York: Oxford University Press.

Murthy, D. (2008). Digital ethnography. *Sociology, 42*(5), 837–855.

Murthy, D. (2011). Emergent digital ethnographic methods for social research. In S. N. Hesse-Biber (Ed.), *The handbook of emergent technologies in social research* (pp. 158–179). New York: Oxford University Press.

Nardi, B. A. (2010). *My life as a night elf priest: An anthropological account of World of Warcraft*. Ann Arbor: University of Michigan Press.

O'Reilly, T. (2005). What is Web 2.0? Design patterns and business models for the next generation of software. Retrieved February 10, 2011, from http://oreilly.com/web2/archive/what-is-web-20.html.

Ong, W. J. (1982). *Orality and literacy: The technologizing of the word*. New York: Methuen.

Orgad, S. S. (2005a). From online to offline and back: Moving from online to offline relationships with research informants. In C. Hine (Ed.), *Virtual methods: Issues in social research on the Internet* (pp. 51–65). Oxford: Berg.

Orgad, S. S. (2005b). *Storytelling online: Talking breast cancer on the Internet*. New York: Peter Lang.

Oulasvirta, A., Lehtonen, E., Kurvinen, E., & Raento, M. (2010). Making the ordinary visible in microblogs. *Personal and Ubiquitous Computing, 14*(3), 237–249.

Paccagnella, L. (1997). Getting the seats of your pants dirty: Strategies for ethnographic research on virtual communities *Journal of Computer-Mediated Communication, 3*(1). http://jcmc.indiana.edu/vol3/issue1/paccagnella.html

Pearce, C. (2009). *Communities of play: Emergent cultures in multiplayer games and virtual worlds*. Cambridge, MA: MIT Press.

Penrod, J. (2003). Getting funded: Writing a successful qualitative small-project proposal. *Qualitative Health Research, 13*(6), 821–832.

Pratt, M. L. (1986). Fieldwork in common places. In J. Clifford & G. E. Marcus (Eds.), *Writing culture: The poetics and politics of ethnography* (pp. 27–50). Berkeley: University of California Press.

Priem, J., & Costello, K. L. (2010). How and why scholars cite on Twitter. *Proceedings of the American Society for Information Science and Technology, 47*(1), 1–4.

Rapley, T. J. (2001). The art(fulness). of open-ended interviewing: Some considerations on analysing interviews. *Qualitative Research, 1*(3), 303–323.

Rheingold, H. (1993). *The virtual community: Homesteading on the electronic frontier* Reading, MA: Addison-Wesley.

Roberts, J. M., & Sanders, T. (2005). Before, during and after: Realism, reflexivity and ethnography. *The Sociological Review, 53*(2), 294–313.

Rybas, N., & Gajjala, R. (2007). Developing cyberethnographic research methods for understanding digitally mediated identities. *Forum Qualitative Sozialforschung/Forum: Qualitative Social Research, 8*(3), Art. 35. Retrieved from http://nbn-resolving.de/urn:nbn:de:0114-fqs0703355

Sandelowski, M., & Barroso, J. (2003). Writing the proposal for a qualitative research methodology project. *Qualitative Health Research, 13*(6), 781–820.

Sanders, T. (2005). Researching the online sex work community. In C. Hine (Ed.), *Virtual methods: Issues in social research on the Internet* (pp. 67–80). Oxford: Berg.

Savage, M., & Burrows, R. (2007). The coming crisis of empirical sociology. *Sociology, 41*(5), 885–899.

Schein, L. (2002). Mapping Hmong media in diasporic space. In F. D. Ginsburg, L. Abu-Lughod, & B. Larkin (Eds.). *Media worlds: Anthropology on new terrains.* (pp. 229–244). Berkeley: University of California Press.

Schneider, S. M., Foot, K. A., & Dougherty, M. (2006). Web Campaigning Digital Supplement V1.0 20061013: Digital supplement goals. Retrieved April 15, 2011, from http://mitpress.mit.edu/books/0262062585/WebCampaigningDigitalSupplement.html%5B%5BDigital%20Supplement%20Goals%5D%5D.

Schroeder, R., & Besten, M. D. (2008). Literary sleuths online: E-Research collaboration on the Pynchon Wiki. *Information, Communication & Society, 11*(2), 167–187.

Scott, S. (2004). Researching shyness: A contradiction in terms? *Qualitative Research, 4*(1), 91–105.

Sculley, J. (1987). *Odyssey. Pepsi to Apple... a journey of adventure, ideas, and the future.* New York: Harper & Row.

Seale, C. (1999). Quality in qualitative research. *Qualitative Inquiry, 5*(4), 465–478.

Seale, C., Charteris-Black, J., MacFarlane, A., & McPherson, A. (2010). Interviews and Internet forums: A comparison of two sources of qualitative data. *Qualitative Health Research, 20*(5), 595–606.

Seymour, W. S. (2001). In the flesh or online? Exploring qualitative research methodologies. *Qualitative Research, 1*(2), 147–168.

Shields, R. (1996). *Cultures of Internet: Virtual spaces, real histories, living bodies.* London: Sage.

Silverman, D. (2006). *Interpreting qualitative data: Methods for analysing talk, text and interaction* (3rd ed.). London: Sage.

Snee, H. (2010). Using blog analysis. Realities Toolkit 10. Retrieved from http://www.manchester.ac.uk/realities/resources/toolkits/blog-analysis/.

Sproull, L., & Kiesler, S. (1986). Reducing social context cues: Electronic mail in organizational communication. *Management Science, 32*(11), 1492–1512.

Sproull, L., & Kiesler, S. (1992). *Connections: New ways of working in the networked organization.* Cambridge, MA: MIT Press.

Strano, M. M. (2008). User descriptions and interpretations of self-presentation through Facebook profile images. *Cyberpsychology: Journal of Psychosocial Research on Cyberspace, 2*(2), Article 1. Retrieved from http://www.cyberpsychology.eu/view.php?cisloclanku=2008110402

Sudweeks, F., & Rafaeli, S. (1996). How do you get a hundred strangers to agree: Computer mediated communication and collaboration. In T.M. Harrison & T.D. Stephen (Eds.), *Computer networking and scholarship in the 21st university* (pp. 115–136). New York: SUNY Press.

Sveinsdottir, T. (2008). Virtual identity as practice: Exploring the relationship between role-players and their characters in the massively multiplayer online game Star Wars Galaxies Doctoral thesis submitted to Department of Sociology, University of Surrey. Retrieved from http://epubs.surrey.ac.uk/2112/1/492978.pdf

Tashakkori, A. (2006). *Mixed methodology: Combining qualitative and quantitative approaches*. Thousand Oaks, CA: Sage.

Taylor, T. L. (2006). *Play between worlds: Exploring online game culture*. Cambridge, MA: MIT Press.

Thelwall, M. (2008). Fk yea I swear: Cursing and gender in MySpace. *Corpora, 3*(1), 83–107. Retrieved from http://www.euppublishing.com/doi/abs/10.3366/E1749503208000087

Underberg, N. M. (2006). Virtual and reciprocal ethnography on the Internet: The East Mims Oral History Project website. *Journal of American Folklore, 119*(473), 301–311.

van Maanen, J. (1988). *Tales of the field: On writing ethnography*. Chicago, IL: University of Chicago Press.

Wakeford, N., & Cohen, K. (2008). Fieldnotes in public: Using blogs for research. In N. Fielding, R. M. Lee, & G. Blank (Eds.), *The Sage handbook of online research methods* (pp. 307–326). London: Sage.

Walther, J. B. (2007). Selective self-presentation in computer-mediated communication: Hyperpersonal dimensions of technology, language, and cognition. *Computers in Human Behavior, 23*(5), 2538–2557.

Ward, M.-H. (2006). *Thoughts on blogging as an ethnographic tool*. The 23rd Annual Conference of the Australasian Society for Computers in Learning in Tertiary Education, University of Sydney, Sydney University Press. Retrieved from http://ascilite.org.au/conferences/sydney06/proceeding/pdf_papers/p164.pdf

Wen, K.-Y., McTavish, F., Kreps, G., Wise, M., & Gustafson, D. (2011). From diagnosis to death: A case study of coping with breast cancer as seen through online discussion group messages. *Journal of Computer-Mediated Communication, 16*(2), 331–361.

Wesch, M. (n.d.). Digital ethnography of YouTube project. Retrieved from http://mediatedcultures.net/youtube.htm.

Wilkinson, D., & Thelwall, M. (2010). Researching personal information on the public web: Methods and ethics. *Social Science Computer Review*. Pre-published August 17, 2010, doi:10.1177/0894439310378979.

Wittel, A. (2000). Ethnography on the move: From field to net to Internet. *Forum Qualitative Sozialforschung/Forum: Qualitative Social Research, 1*(1). Retrieved from http://www.qualitative-research.net/index.php/fqs/article/viewArticle/1131

Wolf, M. (1992). *A thrice-told tale: Feminism, postmodernism and ethnographic responsibility*. Stanford, CA: Stanford University Press.

Woolgar, S. (Ed.). (1988). *Knowledge and reflexivity*. London, Sage.

Yang, X., Wang, L., & Jie, W. (2011). *Guide to e-science: Next generation scientific research and discovery*. London: Springer-Verlag.

Yearley, S. (1981). Textual persuasion: The role of social accounting in the construction of scientific arguments. *Philosophy of the Social Sciences, 11*(3), 409–435.

Zwaanswijk, M., Tates, K., van Dulmen, S., Hoogerbrugge, P., Kamps, W., & Bensing, J. (2007). Young patients', parents', and survivors' communication preferences in paediatric oncology: Results of online focus groups. *BMC Pediatrics, 7*(1), 35. Retrieved from http://www.biomedcentral. com/1471-2431/7/35

INDEX

Note: Page numbers followed by n and *f* refer to notes and figures.

Printed in Great Britain
by Amazon